FACEBOOK MARKETING

FOR SMALL BUSINESS

QUICK START GUIDE

Ready to **create or update your marketing plan?** Turn to **page 18**

It's time to **set up your Facebook Business Page!** Turn to **page 31**

Over a billion people are on Facebook. How will you find your customers? Turn to **page 45** for Facebook Groups.

When you're **ready to start selling,** turn to **page 83** and **create your first Facebook ad.**

We know it works. But how well is it working? **Measure your social engagement** on **page 92**.

Facebook Marketing

FOR SMALL BUSINESS

Easy Strategies
to Engage Your
Facebook Community

By Arnel Leyva
with Natalie Law

TYCHO
PRESS

CONTENTS

INTRODUCTION

If you are reading this book, then you are probably the owner of a small-to-medium business (SMB) interested in learning how to incorporate Facebook marketing into your business plan. You want to increase your revenue by spreading the word about what you have to offer so you can attract more customers and keep them coming back. For you, marketing is not only about getting clicks on your website; it is also about bringing foot traffic into your store or getting phone calls to book the services that you provide.

Facebook Marketing for Small Business will provide everything you need to get started and be successful at Facebook marketing:

- Knowledge of the digital marketing landscape and where Facebook fits
- Marketing tactics based on a plan that uses Facebook as your "hub"
- Instructions on how to set up your Facebook Page and optimize it in order to generate organic (free or unpaid) traffic
- Elements of an effective Facebook Ad and how to set up your first one
- Insight and guidance on how to allocate your ad budget efficiently
- Tutorial on how to drive ROI (return on investment) with both the resources you allocate to organic traffic and the money you spend on paid traffic
- Guide to the Facebook app ecosystem to support your Facebook marketing efforts and ramp up your skills

TOP 10 TIPS FOR FACEBOOK MARKETING

1. Allocate a certain amount of time and money each week toward social media.

2. Use analytics to measure the impact of your social media activity on your business.

3. Develop content regularly to share between your website and Facebook Page.

4. Focus your time and resources on Facebook, your website, and a short list of supporting social media channels, rather than spreading yourself thin across every channel.

5. Drive participation in events at your physical stores through Facebook and supporting social media channels.

6. Define how frequently you can interact with fans on Facebook while balancing your business's operating needs.

7. Use Facebook to support the distribution of content and ideas that positions your company as a thought leader within your industry.

8. Provide clear calls to action that drive Facebook users to your website in order to generate leads.

9. Use information and data that you gather from Facebook users to optimize your business strategy.

10. Use Facebook Ads and Sponsored Stories to help generate organic traffic.

PART

START MARKETING WITH FACEBOOK

O ut of all the traditional and digital marketing channels available to businesses—television, print, display, search, e-mail, and so on—Facebook is the most effective marketing choice for your SMB. Why? Because digital marketing overall is more cost-effective than traditional marketing—you get more exposure for your money. And Facebook marketing, specifically, offers many of the advantages of the other digital marketing channels with the extra advantage of being cost-effective, because of the amplification effect through the word-of-mouth marketing that Facebook users generate. The Facebook fans that your business is able to attract provide free collaborative marketing on your behalf to their network of Facebook friends in an instant.

FACEBOOK: ALL-IN-ONE DIGITAL MARKETING

In the past, large companies had a significant advantage over SMBs when it came to marketing, because large companies' budgets are orders of magnitude bigger than those of smaller ones. But then digital marketing came along and helped to level the playing field. Facebook marketing is still the most democratizing marketing channel for SMBs. But Facebook is only part of your marketing plan—it's not the whole thing.

To deepen your understanding of how Facebook fits into your overall marketing plan, the following sections provide a quick survey of how digital marketing has evolved, how Facebook incorporates or mimics other types of digital marketing, and whether or not it would be worth the investment to include the other types of digital marketing into your overall marketing plan. In the sections that follow, you'll explore four types of marketing:

- E-mail
- Display advertising
- Search marketing
- Social networking

E-MAIL

The first form of direct marketing to efficiently use the Internet was e-mail marketing. Consumers have a long-standing relationship with e-mail marketing and are comfortable with it . . . up to a point. Because of e-mail's efficiency and the practice of buying e-mail lists, it costs very little to spam people. And being a consumer yourself, you know how spam can ruin the perception of a business: Spam is commonly perceived as the second-worst crime on the Internet (the first being identity theft or spying).

E-mail marketing definitely should be an integral part of your marketing plan, but it should be reserved for customers who have freely given their e-mail addresses to you. Consumers become your customers after they have had a transaction with your business by buying your product or service.

That means that you should avoid buying an e-mail list of residents within a certain radius of your business or service area. That's just spamming.

So how can you scale your e-mail list without buying ones that could have been obtained through less-than-official means? Facebook fans. That's right, Facebook can serve as a surrogate for and initiator of e-mail lists. Exactly why and how to do this will be explained later under "Better Than E-mail" (page 71).

DISPLAY ADVERTISING

When Internet display advertising was introduced to the burgeoning online population, it copied the format of print ads in newspapers and magazines. Display ads used to be arbitrary and ineffective—we didn't have the advanced targeting of Web browser cookies, which remember your browsing history, or contextual targeting, which uses the content of a Web page to match the relevance of an ad to the Web page's subject matter. Before paid listings were introduced into the results page of search engines, display advertising was really the only form of digital marketing that could reach the masses.

Facebook is the largest display-advertising platform in the industry. With 1.4 billion users, it surpassed Yahoo as the undisputed leader in this realm a few years ago and remains the king of display. This is why large brands spend so much money on Facebook Ads.

Small-to-medium business owners can use Facebook's enormous size to their advantage, too. Although you, as a small business, may not be trying to make millions of people aware of your product or service, you can target the thousands of people who are looking just for what you have to offer.

SEARCH MARKETING

When search marketing came onto the digital marketing scene, it was hailed as the most effective form of direct one-to-one marketing ever invented. Why? Because consumers could "pull" the information that they wanted directly through the keywords that they entered into the search engine. For the first time, an individual could tell advertisers precisely their intentions at any given moment. Searching is one of the most common things that people do online. And because it is a direct request for information, it is the most accurate barometer of what a consumer wants.

Strategic Thinking

Search marketing needs to be part of your marketing mix, but you have to be strategic about how you use it in order to get the best ROI for your business. When search marketing was introduced, it was the most democratizing form of marketing ever invented—but not anymore. Back then, small businesses could compete in the search results with big brands because of the flatter, less competitive pricing for keywords.

Today, high-value keywords are so expensive that only large companies can afford to buy them, and that is how they like it. This situation allows the companies with the biggest budgets to narrow the scope of their competition. So for businesses on a tight budget, one key to a cost-effective search-marketing plan is to perform research on the keywords that align with your product or service but are more affordable than the most competitive ones.

It's also important to ensure that your website is built to show up in the *organic listings*, which are the largest section of the search results page containing unpaid listings. Your site should also be updated regularly with fresh content to keep it relevant as judged by the search-engine algorithms.

Remember, Facebook itself is considered the Internet within the Internet, a community serving as the main online experience for a large portion of the Internet population. A Facebook Page can be seen as a business's website within this vast online community. An entire section of this book is dedicated to telling you exactly how you can optimize your "Facebook website." See part 2, starting on page 40.

Although search marketing is not the main subject of this book, search marketing's best practices can be applied to optimize your Facebook Page to keep it current within News Feeds.

News Feeds

A user's News Feed behaves kind of like automatically updated search results. The user doesn't choose what these results show. Instead, the content that Facebook uses to populate each user's News Feed is based on the preferences in each user's profile—for example, people, businesses, and organizations that they already follow, brands from which they buy, and their network of friends.

SOCIAL NETWORKING

The popularity of social networks and the trove of personal data that users freely provide in their profiles make this online obsession a formidable form of personalized marketing. These facts apply to Facebook in particular. This phenomenon also provides consumers with communication channels to give feedback directly to businesses and tell others about their experiences. Unlike search marketing, *consumer intent*—what a person wants at any particular moment—is indirect and thus inferred. So, it is more akin to display advertising rather than search marketing. This is due to the massive amounts of personal data that people willingly provide to Facebook and other social networks. This practice creates the most accurate consumer profiles in the history of marketing.

Equally, the integration of other social media channels—like Twitter through Hootsuite, as well as PayPal, which can be used as a social media–payment platform—provides the means to increase the visibility of your Facebook presence and facilitate online conversions of followers to customers.

Not only should Facebook be the hub of your social media plan, but it should also *drive* your overall marketing plan. Using this as your foundation will position you to get the best return on your marketing investment. Implementing this strategy goes beyond creating and optimizing your Facebook Page. Facebook is now an ecosystem of features and apps. There are best practices in leveraging the different faces of Facebook to maximize benefits for your business. Explanations and examples of these practices are at the core of this book.

POWER TO THE CONSUMER

As a business owner, you already have been exposed to many marketing concepts. You most likely know the difference between traditional marketing and advertising (television, radio, and print) and social media marketing (Facebook is the star of this solar system). You may also know the term *target market*—the people who want your product or service. They are the ones who are the "targets" of your marketing. The word *target* holds the key to understanding the difference between how traditional marketers treated their consumers compared to how social media marketers treat their audience. Knowing why you need to approach your consumers differently through social media and how to do this will define whether you fail or succeed in your Facebook marketing endeavor.

POTENTIAL PARTNERS, NOT TARGETS

Why does marketing lingo borrow heavily from military terminology? Because traditional marketers from the *Mad Men* days treated consumers as "targets" to conquer. But now consumers are armed with military-grade mobile technology and massive reach through social media platforms, which means they can fire back. Businesses that act badly and do not keep their promises are in consumers' crosshairs—in an instant, consumers can tell all to their Facebook friends or Twitter followers about a bad experience with a business. So businesses must look for ways to invite and integrate consumers into the marketing process. You should see consumers as *potential partners* who will market to their friends on your behalf.

Even with the brands that they love, consumers want some power, some control over product and messaging development. In short, modern consumers, emboldened by technological devices and services, want a balanced and reciprocal relationship with the businesses that can support and enhance their lifestyles.

The worst and best examples of how consumers can hurt and help the public's perception of a business come from two stories about the way in which social media affected big brands like United Airlines and Frito-Lay.

United Breaks Guitars

Although you as an SMB owner operate far from the scale of United Airlines, this story serves as a poignant lesson in how bad customer service can have a sizable effect on the value of your business.

Musician Dave Carroll handed in his $3,500 Taylor guitar as baggage during a United Airlines flight. When he arrived at his destination, he discovered that the guitar was severely damaged. So he filed a claim, but United Airlines told him that he was ineligible for compensation because he did not make the claim within the company's standard 24-hour time frame. In response, Carroll wielded his musical creativity and the power of social media—he wrote a song and made a music video about his experience, uploading it to YouTube. He posted the video on July 6, 2009. Within one day, it amassed 150,000 views. United Airlines quickly contacted him and apologized by saying they hoped to right the wrong.

But Bob Taylor, owner of Taylor Guitars, already had offered Carroll two guitars and other props for his second video about the incident. Carroll's song climbed to Number 1 on the iTunes Music Store the week after its release. United Airlines' compensation offer of $3,000 was too late, so they donated it to the Thelonious Monk Institute of Jazz as a gesture of goodwill. But that gesture failed to undo the damage done to the company's image. Within four days of the release of the YouTube video, United Airlines' stock price fell 10 percent, which translated into a loss of $180 million in market value.

As of February 2015, the original video has garnered 14 million views.

Frito-Lay's "Do Us a Flavor" Contest

To envision just how successful a partnership between marketers and consumers can be, no matter how big or small the business, look at Lay's "Do Us a Flavor" Tastes of America contest. In this campaign, consumers entered suggestions for new potato chip flavors and a chance to win $1 million. It quickly became a pop-culture phenomenon, with millions of entries from every corner of the United States. The contest entries resulted in crowd-sourced product ideas.

The Lay brand celebrated fans' flavor ideas by creating real-time, personalized content shared through Facebook, Instagram, and Twitter. These Big Three all offer *two-way* marketing channels that allow consumers to tell brands what they want. This is in stark contrast to the *one-way* communication that traditional media such as television, radio, and print offers. As a result, Lay reaped the benefits of word-of-mouth marketing. The dynamic content generated through these interactions and distributed through social media effectively amounted to contestants freely marketing Lay's products to other consumers.

The contest generated prepublicity for new products that consumers helped create, accomplishing this through consumers' most trusted marketing source—user-generated content on social media.

SHOW THEM YOU CARE

One way or another, everyone is a consumer. Consumers want to express themselves to businesses in order to receive the services that they want, delivered how they want them.

The traditional marketing approach, with its militaristic view of consumers as targets, has been cut down by social media. So now the most popular marketing catchphrases are "relevancy" (give consumers what they want) and "authenticity" (be honest about the value that your business provides). Taken together, these catchphrases point to a sentiment of "caring"—placing the best interest of customers ahead of your business's own balance sheet.

This is an era in which customers who are treated badly can upload a video to YouTube and decrease a corporation's value by hundreds of millions of dollars. Customers can market new products on your behalf to millions of their collective friends. The take-home message is this: Business owners must always bear in mind that truly caring for customers is the most effective way to drive revenue.

CREATE YOUR MARKETING PLAN

The *purchase funnel* provides a framework for developing your marketing plan. Digital marketers argue that the classic purchase funnel is no longer applicable because of the circuitous nature of modern digital life, with multiple screens and a seemingly infinite amount of media vying for our attention at all times of the day. But life—personal and commercial—has always been circuitous. So, the classic purchase funnel continues to distill the roundabout path people take to find and get the things they need and want in life. And it works great for creating a marketing plan.

What follows is an overview of the nine sections required to build your marketing plan:

1. Executive Summary
2. Target Market (Potential Partners)
3. USP (Unique Selling Proposition) or Value Proposition

4. Positioning and Pricing

5. Distribution Plan

6. Offers and Deals

7. Marketing Materials

8. Marketing Channels

9. Financial Projections

Everything covered in *Facebook Marketing for Small Business* builds on these nine sections.

You can build or refine your marketing plan by performing these tasks:

- List the sections that you need to create

- Describe the content of each section

- Read the subsequent sections of this book to discover how Facebook marketing and supporting digital channels apply to the sections of your plan

Bear in mind that your marketing plan is a living document. It needs to be updated as your business evolves and you learn new things to drive it further. So this part of the book is not merely for those business owners who need to create a marketing plan from scratch. It is also for those business owners who already have a marketing plan developed and need to hone it.

1. EXECUTIVE SUMMARY

This section will be the last one you do though it will appear at the beginning of your plan. As the name implies, it contains the summary of the other sections of your marketing plan. Some of you may ask, why even bother? Your Executive Summary will be crucial in providing your constituents—such as employees and advisors—with an overview of your plan. It will serve as your team's call to action.

2. TARGET MARKET (POTENTIAL PARTNERS)

This part of your plan defines the type of people you want to buy your products or to whom you want to provide your services. It explains their *demographic profile* (age, gender, and so on) and *psychographic makeup* (their interests) by describing their wants and needs in terms of your products or services. This is a vital exercise, as doing this will allow you to understand which marketing and advertising channels you should use to reach your consumers and develop the messages in a manner that they will understand.

For example, you decided to read this book because you know that many of your customers use Facebook. But with approximately 1.4 billion users, who doesn't use it? Knowing your potential partners will allow you to wield the power of Facebook effectively, because with this knowledge you can identify the Facebook Groups that your consumers likely have joined and decide whether or not to spend resources marketing on Instagram.

As an SMB, your target market necessarily will be a *"niche"*—a small subsection of the mass market. How to successfully define and target your niche is explained on page 26.

3. USP (UNIQUE SELLING PROPOSITION) OR VALUE PROPOSITION

Defining your *unique selling proposition* or *value proposition* allows you to communicate the essence of what distinguishes your company from its competitors and the value that you provide to your consumers. There is an ongoing debate among the marketing literati over whether the USP and value proposition are the same thing or two completely different things. For the purposes of an SMB, the USP and value proposition should be treated as one and the same.

You need to answer these three questions in one sentence in order to determine your USP:

- What do you do?
- For whom?
- And why?

An example of a global brand's USP is Apple's: They're the simplest computer to use in the world, so everyone can experience technology's benefits. Or a small business like a dry cleaner might say that it provides a high-quality, same-day service so that the neighborhood it serves can enjoy those conveniences.

Your USP will be the foundation of all the content that you create. It will be the first thing that people see on your website and your Facebook Page.

4. POSITIONING AND PRICING

It is imperative that you align the strategies that you use for positioning and pricing. If you want to position your company as a leading brand in your industry, undercutting the prices of your competitors will not make sense to anyone and will turn them off. For small businesses, this strategy is not so simple. You must have relatively affordable prices to attract new customers even if you position your business as a premier establishment, so research your competition to ensure that your prices are competitive and fit with your positioning strategy.

5. DISTRIBUTION PLAN

In this section, you will describe in detail how you will deliver your goods or services to your customers. Will they buy directly from your store or your website? Will they buy from distributors, or will you provide your products through other retailers as well? If you are a local business that sells exclusively through your store, this section of your plan can include a strategy to start selling online through your website and Facebook Page.

6. OFFERS AND DEALS

Offers are special deals that help you acquire new customers and retain current customers. While the success of your business is not necessarily predicated on giving offers, using them is an effective way to grow your customer base more quickly. The types of offers and deals that work best on Facebook are detailed on page 97.

7. MARKETING MATERIALS

These are the specific pieces of collateral that you will use to promote your business. Marketing materials comprise any content that you will develop to be distributed through digital and traditional marketing channels, including the following:

Digital

- Website
- Facebook Page (and other social media profiles)
- Thought leadership blogs/articles
- Digital ads/copy

Traditional

- Business cards
- Brochures
- Print ads
- Catalogs

Suggestions on which types of marketing materials you should develop, based on the right digital strategy for your business, are weaved throughout this book. At the very least, you should have a website, Facebook Page, and business cards.

8. MARKETING CHANNELS

All the work you have done so far leads to this important section—how you will reach your consumers. This is the longest section of your marketing plan. It contains the deepest explanations of any of the sections thus far. Because this is a book on Facebook marketing, the focus should be on digital marketing channels.

Traditional Practices

Traditionally, large companies could spend more money on outbound marketing techniques like television, print, and direct mail. This advantage, founded on economies of scale, meant more people were aware of what the large companies had to offer compared to small, local competitors. Traditional outbound marketing started the consumer's journey down the purchase funnel, the predictable path that consumers take toward making a transaction with a business.

Successful small businesses have thrived on word of mouth to help promote their products or services. With digital marketing and social media, small businesses have the ability to use cost-effective tools to increase word of mouth while decreasing the need for expensive outbound advertising.

Word of Mouth

Getting to the point where a customer will tell a friend about your business—the essence of *word of mouth*—is the true goal of the purchase funnel. Turning a customer into your brand advocate is the goal, as that is the point of marketing collaboration. This result turns your customers into your salespeople. Customers perpetuate the ROI that you originally made to acquire them. At this point they are generating awareness for you by telling their friends and acquaintances about you and your business.

There are four aspects of marketing channels:

- Brand awareness
- Consideration
- Transaction
- Loyalty and advocacy

Stage One: Brand Awareness Consumers search for businesses, products, and services that have the ability to meet their basic needs and desires. Traditionally, this meant responding to a television commercial or newspaper/magazine ad or flipping through the Yellow Pages. Today it is more common for this search to start on a search engine, through exposure to display ads, or via e-mails from deal websites. The term *discovery* also is attached to brand awareness. This phenomenon happens through the online version of word of mouth, such as recommendations from Facebook friends that show up in a News Feed.

A list of channels and media that you can take advantage of at this stage include the following:

- Facebook Ads
- Instagram
- Twitter Ads
- Directory listings (Yelp, YP, etc.)

Stage Two: Consideration Once a consumer has been made aware of the possible options out there, they move to the consideration stage and begin to filter the results by conditions like incentives, location, recommendations, and ratings.

The list of channels, media, and features that you can take advantage of at this stage include the following:

- Reviews from Facebook fans
- Likes from Facebook fans
- Search retargeting/Facebook remarketing
- Twitter followers

Stage Three: Transaction Once consumers decide on a preference, they enter the conversion stage where a transaction is highly likely. At this point of the consumer journey, you will want to make it as easy as possible for people to decide on your business to deliver the product or service that they need.

The list of channels, media, and features that you can take advantage of at this stage include the following:

- Facebook campaign with coupons and offers
- E-mail campaign
- E-commerce integration

Stage Four: Loyalty and Advocacy After consumers make a transaction and become your customers, you are given the opportunity to further the relationship and turn them into loyal brand advocates. In some versions of the purchase funnel, loyalty and advocacy are separate stages. But even though reality dictates that not all satisfied customers become advocates of your brand, doing the things that make customers loyal tends also to make them vocal brand advocates.

During the loyalty phase, you have an opportunity to build information about your client base by looking at data that you have collected on them. Store this information in a customer-relationship management (CRM) system—no matter how rudimentary—for further analysis. You can use this data to connect authentically and more deeply with your loyal customers. Link ongoing marketing efforts to your customers' actual needs and desires, as opposed to doing the guesswork involved in earlier stages of the purchase funnel.

As a consumer yourself, think about where you spend money. Consider the ways that you search and interact with the businesses that have earned your loyalty. Remember those that have turned you off by their actions (or inaction). You can see that your own business's survival in the digital age goes well beyond having great products and providing superior services.

Great customer service begins with making it simple for your consumers to find, understand, and transact with you, regardless of where they may be looking. While there is a start to the purchase funnel, there is no end, because the purchase funnel is truly a circular customer cycle that defines the success or failure of your business.

The following channels, media, and features that you would use to accomplish loyalty will in turn achieve advocacy and vice versa:

- Exclusive Facebook fans campaign
- Exclusive E-mail campaigns integrated with third-party e-mail platforms
- Instagram campaigns
- Facebook Insights

9. FINANCIAL PROJECTIONS

This is the final part of your marketing plan. Your projections should include all the information documented in your marketing plan—the budget you will need to implement the plan and the ROI that you expect. Of course your financial projections will never be 100 percent accurate, but they will allow you to set goals for your company.

Based on the previous sections of your marketing plan, your financial projections should be calculated using the following components:

- Size of target market
- Cost and margin of your pricing strategy
- Effects of your distribution plan on your margins
- Cost of offers/deals and expected leads generated
- Costs of marketing materials
- Costs of paid advertising and expected leads generated
- Resource costs of organic marketing and expected leads generated
- Projected sales revenues

IDENTIFYING YOUR NICHE

During the exercise in developing your marketing plan, you had to identify your target market and then define your unique selling proposition to them. Whether or not you were aware of it, you were involved in "niche marketing." You were doing the same thing that car manufacturers do when developing new cars for their product line that targets certain market segments based on age, gender, and income. Just as you were doing the same thing that a local organic farmer might do when devising a new yogurt product based on certain interests and lifestyles.

NICHE MARKETING

A *niche market* is a segment of the mass market. It can be further divided into subsegments of a market segment. For example, the fashion market is massive. Within it, there are women's fashions, men's fashions, and children's fashions. Drill down further and you get luxury items, maternity wear, teen fashions, and baby wear. Go even further and you come to subniches like eco-friendly clothing made of organic material that you can wash in a bathtub while traveling because they will dry quickly hanging from a towel bar. Some of these subniches can be highly profitable, spanning across demographics and psychographics.

Whether your business is massive or small, starting narrow allows you to define your particular niche and market your product or services to that segment of the market. Many business owners view the idea of starting narrow as a disadvantageous strategy. They believe it will cut profit margins or limit sales. But there are three main reasons why focusing on a niche is the most effective strategy for businesses of any size:

1. Creating a product or service that does all things for all people is the kiss of death. This is an impossible approach that will suck the resources dry of even the largest, most well-funded organizations, because it is impossible.

2. Serving a niche market means you can mitigate the risk and exposure of the time and resources that you need to invest, as the market that you are serving can be tailored to a manageable size relative to your available resources.

3. Identifying the right niche means that there is enough demand and money in that market, while having fewer competitors.

If you can precisely define your niche market, the likelihood that the marketing messages stemming from your unique selling proposition will resonate with this market will be higher. Then, you'll be able to turn this audience into fans who will not only buy into your value proposition, but also rave about your business to others.

RESEARCHING PROFITABLE NICHE MARKETS

Researching profitable niche markets usually is an exercise for entrepreneurs looking to start a new business. However, it is also worthwhile for the majority of you who are reading this book. You can use this same approach to precisely define your target market. The methods are similar to those that you would apply to reach your potential partners through digital marketing.

Identify Your Audience

It is probably a safe bet to say that you are passionate about the reason that you created your business. Perhaps you were part of a community that shared the same interests, and you saw a market for building a viable business. Without knowing any better, you used a best practice in starting a niche business. That is, you first chose a niche audience that you understood deeply rather than identifying a product to promote.

Products come and go, but niches and their lifestyles are here to stay. Rather than struggling to find ideas for products, you have a better grasp of the types of products you should be promoting, because they align with your niche audience's needs.

SUCCESS STORY

Digital Marketing Is More Than a Static Page

ADVERTISER PROFILE
NAME: Rainier Envoys
TYPE OF BUSINESS: Independent marketing and design agency
MONTHLY FACEBOOK AD SPEND: $5000, but dramatically decreased over time while increasing organic leads

The owner of this SMB thought she was doing digital marketing from the first day she opened business. But after creating a marketing plan that started with Facebook as the hub, she looked back and realized that all she really had when she started was a static website that was not much more than a digital brochure. When she started the business, she focused on outbound (or traditional) marketing—newspaper and Yellow Pages ads, direct mail brochures, and even neighborhood telemarketing—which was expensive and took a lot of time from the company's staff. This SMB owner found out rather quickly that she could not scale the business by relying on traditional marketing. So the owner decided to focus on inbound (or digital) marketing.

KEYWORDS, NEEDS, AND EXPECTATIONS: The business started by using Google AdWords to generate leads. Soon, it discovered that the most valuable keywords for its services were extremely competitive and thus expensive. This drove up the cost-per-lead and killed the marketing budget. As a consumer, the owner noticed that her needs and expectations when researching, shopping, and generally stumbling on the products and services that she needed in her life had changed. The same was true for other consumers in general:

- Consumers expect cool and informative content when they land on business websites.
- Websites that show up at or near the top of organic search results not only have cool and informative content, but also are updated with fresh content often.
- Display ads for SMBs often show up on Facebook Profile Pages.
- Facebook Pages of businesses with cool, informative, and fresh content reuse the content from their websites and include links to longer-form fresh content.
- Facebook News Feeds regularly include these types of businesses.

FACEBOOK ADS AND FACEBOOK PAGES: The owner recognized how Facebook Ads can be managed cost-effectively to drive brand awareness for her SMB. Furthermore, she saw how great and fresh content on a website in tandem with a Facebook Page drives organic optimization on search engines and Facebook News Feeds once consumers discover one or the other, creating a virtuous cycle value from the initial ad spend.

It usually takes a few months to start driving traffic from organic marketing efforts. So, the owner used Facebook Ads to serve two purposes:

1. Generate initial brand awareness.
2. Drive paid leads while the content creation being distributed on the website and Facebook Page gained momentum.

This practice is par for the course; businesses normally spend more on paid advertising in those initial months of brand building and decrease ad spending as organic traffic ramps up.

THOUGHT LEADERSHIP: As the owner did more research, she realized that companies publishing thought-provoking and relevant content were building thought leadership in their industries. They came to be recognized as trusted sources of the industry zeitgeist. So the owner set out to turn her business into a thought leader in the SMB's industry through content creation and distribution.

CONTENT CREATION STRATEGY: For global brands and local business alike, a viable content-creation strategy needs to meet these two criteria:

1. Fitting with how the business wants its brand to be perceived
2. Solving a consumer need during the decision-making process, and ideally, covering some post-purchase needs at the same time.

THE STRATEGY THAT THE OWNER EMPLOYED WAS A SIMPLE ONE: She wanted consumers to view the SMB as forward-thinking while never leaving its customers behind in the pursuit of what's new. So she put herself inside the heads of her customers. The owner underscored the necessity of answering essential questions that customers might have. Providing answers and tips to actual and potential customers' questions and concerns has been the driving force of the SMB's digital marketing success.

MARKETING COSTS: TRADITIONAL VS. DIGITAL: The owner compared her business's traditional marketing costs to its digital channels. When she first started, her marketing budget was dedicated mainly to traditional marketing and a portion to Facebook Ads and Google AdWords. Once she implemented her digital marketing plan and the organic leads started rolling in, the company was able to reduce ad spend by more than half. Even with such a significant decrease in spending, the SMB enjoyed its best year ever for new business leads and repeat customers.

MAKING TIME TO DRIVE ROI: Small-to-medium business owners need to spend their time actually running their businesses. But to drive further success, they also must carve out time for marketing. So how does the SMB owner allocate the time needed to create compelling content and update the company's website and Facebook Page? She allocates approximately 10 to 20 hours per week between herself and her team. This amount of time lets her create a couple of 200-word blogs, daily Facebook posts, a few new photos per week, as well as two videos per month—all of which are updated on her business's website and Facebook Page. This allocation also allows her to study analytics for website traffic and Facebook in order to map out future improvements.

Find Your Niche Market Keywords

Keywords are the currency of the Internet. You use them to find what you're looking for on search engines and in social media. Finding the keywords that your audience uses to research topics related to your niche market will allow you to identify the words to use in the marketing content that you will create. This will drive the optimization of your website and Facebook Page so that they show up when your audience is searching.

Google AdWords' Keyword Planner is a free and simple tool that you can use after signing up for an account. Use it to identify the keywords that your audience is using to research products, services, solutions, and information related to your niche market. The most important data to pay attention to is the monthly search volume. The higher the search volume, the bigger the market. Anything more than 1,000 exact match searches per month is worthwhile. Having said that, some niche markets may have smaller monthly volumes but still can be highly profitable, especially for high-margin products with low competition.

SETTING UP YOUR FACEBOOK BUSINESS PAGE

Facebook continually evolves by changing and adding product features, which means the steps for setting up a Facebook Page change over time. Having said that, there are essential components in setting up a Facebook Page, and here they are.

Create a Facebook Profile. Do this step if you do not have a Facebook personal profile. If you already have one, go to the next step.

- You should have your personal Facebook profile set up before creating a Facebook Page for your business. If you are going to advertise and promote your business on Facebook without a personal profile, you will run into limitations by having a business-only Facebook Page.

- Go to Facebook.com to do this. Once you have logged in, you can go to step 2 to create your Facebook Page. Your Page will be associated with your personal profile, but they are managed and operated separately. This means your personal information does not show up on your Facebook Page.

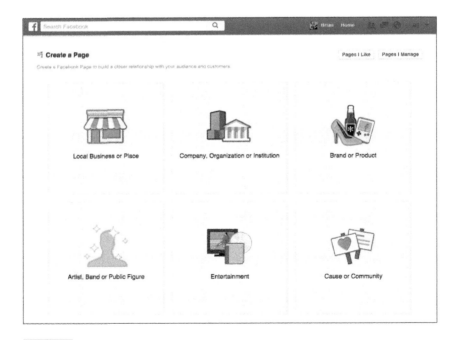

facebook

Email or Phone   Password   Log In
Keep me logged in   Forgot your password?

Sign Up

It's free and always will be.

First name   Last name

Email or mobile number

Re-enter email or mobile number

New password

Birthday

Month ♦ Day ♦ Year ♦   Why do I need to provide my birthday?

○ Female   ○ Male

By clicking Sign Up, you agree to our Terms and that you have read our Data Policy, including our Cookie Use.

Sign Up

FIGURE 1

Search Facebook   Brian Home

≡ **Create a Page**   Pages I Like   Pages I Manage

Create a Facebook Page to build a closer relationship with your audience and customers.

Local Business or Place   Company, Organization or Institution   Brand or Product

Artist, Band or Public Figure   Entertainment   Cause or Community

FIGURE 2

Create a Facebook Page.

- Go to Facebook.com/pages/create.php.

- Survey the main categories of the Pages and decide which one best reflects your business, then click one of the boxes to select the main category on which you decided.

- Then browse the subcategories in the drop-down menus until you find one that you think most closely reflects your business.

- If you have a physical location for your business or a defined service area, select Local Business or Place. Otherwise, skip this step, or else Facebook will automatically make your Page into a Place.

- Enter the name of your Page into the box just under the Category menu. This should be your brand name. Moreover, including keywords that describe your product or service in the Page title can help it appear in relevant Facebook searches. The Page name limit is 70 characters.

  » Facebook automatically capitalizes the first word of the Page name. Another important page-naming rule is that unconventional capitalizations like "MyBusiness" are not allowed. If your business name officially is rendered like that, you can file a petition so it shows up as such, but only after you have created your Page under the enforced rules.

  » Note that you can change the name of your Page name until you have amassed 200 fans or likes.

- Select the box for "I agree to Facebook Pages Terms," and then click Get Started.

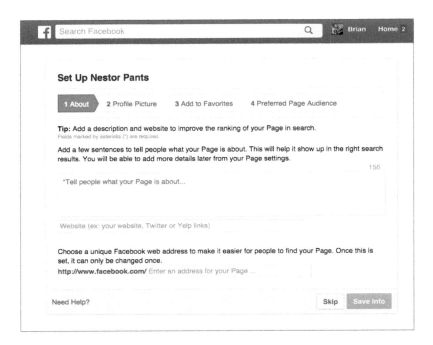

FIGURE 3

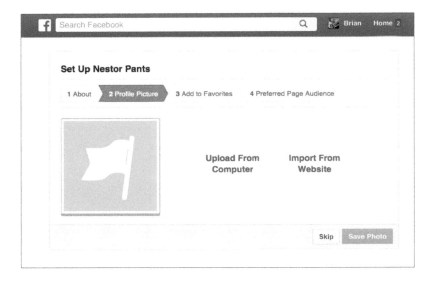

FIGURE 4

Add your basic About information. The About Page contains several sections in which you describe the value that your business provides to consumers. Enter the relevant text into these sections.

- As your Facebook Page is a reflection of your website (and vice versa), this is a good place to reuse descriptive content from your website. Search engines will index your About Page just as they index your website. So, be sure that you have defined your value proposition; how your business is positioned against competitors and aligned with partners; and the benefits that you provide to consumers. Sprinkle these with the keywords that describe your business.

- Note that 155 characters of the About information will appear directly on your timeline underneath your Cover Photo. So be sure that the first 155 characters of your business description capture the essence of your business's value to consumers.

- To ensure that your Facebook Page and website are linked in a virtuous cycle of organic goodness, you should include a link to your website in the About field. Furthermore, you can add other websites that are associated with your business from other social sites by clicking the Add Another Site link.

- Click the Yes radio button that you are representing a real business, and then click Save Info.

Add your Profile Picture. Browse to find the image that you want to use and then upload it.

- The ideal size for this photo is 180 by 180 pixels, but larger photos also are acceptable.

- After you have uploaded your Profile Photo, click Next.

BUILDING YOUR PAGE

Like your own Facebook Page. You will be prompted to like your own Page. This is not a required step.

Invite your e-mail contacts. Best practice dictates that you should build out your Facebook Page with good content before you do this. Instead, you can use your e-mail service to create an invitation.

Share something. Facebook prompts you to share your first status update.
As stated in the previous step, you will not be ready to invite people to your Page until it looks good. Plus, best practice dictates that you already have multiple status updates on your timeline before inviting people to like your Page. This gives people a chance to see the type of content that you will be sharing and gives your request to like your Page authenticity.

Add a Cover Photo. Click the Add a Cover button and then click Upload Photo. Browse and select the photo that you want to use, position it on your Page, and then click Save Changes.

- If you want to change the Cover Photo, hover over the bottom-right corner of the Cover Photo area and select the option you need.

- An image is worth a thousand words, so a high-quality Cover Photo that represents your business is essential. The minimum size for a Cover Photo is 399 pixels wide. Optimally, your Cover Photo should be 851 pixels wide by 315 pixels tall.

- Facebook's Cover Photo terms say that only 20 percent of the photo can contain text. This is a prudent rule, as your Cover Photo should graphically represent your business in a vibrant way. You can choose to include text such as calls to action, websites, or addresses. Keep in mind that too much or misplaced text can decrease the power of the image.

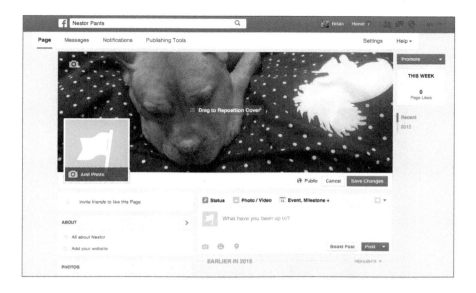

FIGURE 5

Review your permissions. In the Settings Panel, go to Edit Page > Manage Permissions. In general, the default settings are acceptable for a new Page. Here you can change the Moderation and Profanity Filter and the status of your Message button.

- When you reach the point of having a very active Facebook community around your brand, you will need to be just as active in managing spam and profanity. This is a good problem to have—it means that your Page has a lot of engaged followers.

- The Message button is on by default. This means people can send messages to your Page. Leaving it on involves managing another inbox. Turning it off would require visitors to contact you through your business e-mail address.

PART

REFINE YOUR STRATEGY

N ow that you have created your Facebook Page, it is time to get it ready for the big leagues.

In order to understand how optimizing your Facebook Page will help people discover it when they search on Facebook, first we need to consider the best practices that are shared between social optimization and search optimization.

OPTIMIZING YOUR FACEBOOK PAGE

TEXT, IMAGES, VIDEO, AND SHARING

Sharing *content*—text, images, and videos—is the main way to appear in search results. The most effective method of attracting and then engaging your target audience is by posting quality, relevant content.

Follow these steps to upload videos to your Facebook Page:

1. Click the small Facebook icon at the top of your News Feed or Timeline.
2. Click Upload Photos/Video and then browse to choose a video file from your computer.
3. Click Post.

Note that your video will need to be processed before others can see it on Facebook. When it is ready to view, you will receive a notification. Then you need to go to the video on your Facebook Page and click Edit to add a title, tag friends, and choose a thumbnail for the video.

Tips:

- Make sure the content is related to your business.
- Use high-resolution images and well-edited videos all the time.
- Encourage interaction with your content—post updates that compel people to like or comment on it, and request that people share or tag photos and videos for something in return.
- Create content that informs and educates people about your industry or gives them exclusive insight into your business.

POSTING A YOUTUBE VIDEO ON YOUR FACEBOOK PAGE

For those of you who prefer to upload videos to your YouTube channel and share them from your Facebook Page, there are two methods to do this:

Method 1: Using Embedded Code

1. Go to the YouTube video that you want to post on your Facebook Page.
2. Click the Share button below the bottom-left corner of the video.
3. Click the Embed button; a text field will display the embed code for the video.
4. Copy the code.
5. Log into your Facebook Page in another browser page or tab.
6. Paste the code into the What's On Your Mind? text field at the top of your Facebook Page's Timeline; once a video thumbnail appears below the code, you can delete the code and replace it with text that describes the video.
7. Click Post to share the video on your Facebook Page.

Method 2: Using Share to Facebook

1. Go to the YouTube video that you want to post to your Facebook Page.
2. Click the Share button below the bottom-left corner of the video.
3. Click the Facebook icon below the bottom-right corner of the video; a Facebook window will open containing the thumbnail of the video. Note that if you have not logged into your Facebook account already, a login prompt will appear for you to enter your credentials to log into Facebook.
4. The Share to Facebook window will appear. Click the drop-down menu in the top-right corner and select Share on a Page You Manage. Your Facebook Business Page will appear as an option—make sure that this page is selected.

FIGURE 6

5. Type text that you want to accompany the video into the "Say something about this" field.

6. Click Post to Facebook to post the video to your Facebook Page.

NEWS FEEDS: THE INDIRECT SEARCH RESULTS

Ever wonder how Facebook decides if and when a post appears in your News Feed? It all has to do with their proprietary algorithm, EdgeRank. As a business owner, it's important that you understand how EdgeRank works. That way, you can do the right things to show up in your fans' News Feeds.

EdgeRank

Digital marketing research has shown that on average only 16 percent of all fans of a brand will see that brand's posts in their News Feeds. Why would Facebook design EdgeRank to gate posts this way? Wouldn't you as a user want to see the updates from the people and brands you love . . . and even those you just like? Think of it this way—if Facebook did not exert some automated way to control which posts appear in people's News Feeds, then those people who have liked hundreds of Facebook Pages would be drowning in daily updates on their timelines. Think of EdgeRank as a spam monitor.

The following are the main controls that EdgeRank uses to figure out who receives which updates:

Affinity: A measurement of the strength of the relationship between the user and the creator; the closer the relationship, the higher the score. You might think this means that your sibling would be more likely to see your post than that guy from high school who tracked you down a couple months ago. Not necessarily, but very likely, in that there is a higher probability that you will have more engagement—communicating more often—with your sibling than with that other guy. The same rule holds true for Facebook Pages that users have liked—EdgeRank measures the ones with which users engage more often as having a stronger affinity.

Weight: Different types of posts are weightier than others; the heavier the weight, the higher the score. There is a distinct order in the types of content and the weight they each carry—photos and videos carry the most weight, followed by links and plain-text updates being the lightest.

Time Decay: Posts continually lose their value as they age. So EdgeRank keeps your News Feed fresh and relevant by neglecting older posts. Having said that, the age of a post is relative to how often a user logs into his or her Facebook account—posts age faster for daily users than for those who log in less often.

Improving Scores

Here are five ways you can improve your Facebook Page's EdgeRank score:

Short but sweet wins the day. Shorter posts get more likes, comments, and shares than longer ones.

Tell your story in pictures. Photos and videos get more engagement than plain-text posts.

Invite interaction. Asking people for their opinions or to fill in blanks increases interaction.

Post regularly. Increase the chances that your post will appear in News Feeds through volume, but do not inundate your fans and make sure you have something good to say.

Find your fans' rhythm. Post at different times of the day and find the times during which your fans are the most active. You can figure this out by using Facebook Insights, which is covered on page 51.

OPTIMIZING FOR MOBILE DEVICES

On many social media platforms, such as Twitter, YouTube, and LinkedIn, the way that the content is formatted is similar across the desktop, tablet, and mobile worlds. But Facebook's user experience is very different depending on the device it is being accessed on. Because more than 50 percent of Facebook's traffic comes through mobile devices, you must always bear in mind that you need to optimize the content that you post to Facebook for mobile devices. This is even more important for local businesses, as local searches represent the highest-converting traffic, and the majority of these types of searches are performed on mobile devices.

Here are a few approaches and best practices for Facebook mobile optimization.

THE TIMELINE IS YOUR BEST MOBILE FRIEND

For those business owners who are also avid Facebook users and long for the pre-Timeline days, bear in mind that mobile- and tablet-user interfaces were the primary drivers of Facebook's Timeline design. Mobile devices and tablets employ a vertical and layered format to move content along. So optimizing for the Timeline is in essence optimizing for mobile.

This means using images, videos, and questions to drive interaction. By following these best practices, you also will be optimizing for EdgeRank.

TEXT YOUR TEXT

Text messaging was the original phenomenon that trained people to write messages within character limits. Twitter's microblogging made people express themselves with even more precision (or with more acronyms, depending on your perspective). The best practice for optimizing Facebook posts for mobile devices is the same as it is with Twitter and ultimately will help your EdgeRank score—keep your posts as short and sweet as a tweet. This approach allows all smartphones to display most of the text in your post.

MOBILE SEO

Remember that your Facebook Page is only one facet of your brand presence. It is a doorway to your website and ultimately to the door of your store. So optimizing your brand presence for mobile users means ensuring that there are as many doorways to your business as possible in search engine results, and that the information for which mobile users are searching is displayed front and center in these doorways.

Tips:

Make your website mobile friendly. Consumers increasingly turn away from websites that are not mobile friendly. Just think of the last time you clicked the link to a website and could not read it because it was merely a shrunken, difficult-to-read version of the desktop site. If you did not have your website created using responsive Web design—an approach to Web design that provides an optimal viewing experience across devices—then you should invest in having your website refitted. Otherwise, you might turn off prospective customers.

List your business. The typical local search on a smartphone will take consumers to one of three places: an ad, a map listing, or a third-party directory listing. Since this section is about organic optimization, let us put paid advertising on the backburner. Just as important as having a mobile-friendly website, you need to have an accurate profile in Google and Bing Maps, as well as in Yelp, YP, and industry-specific directories like Avvo for lawyers.

Display operating information prominently. Industry research shows that consumers search for operating information, such as hours of operation, store address, and directions, predominantly on their mobile devices. As an SMB owner, you must ensure this type of information is present and current in your Google and Bing Maps profiles, as well as in your local directory profiles, because these links are more likely to be selected in mobile search results than a link to your website.

FACEBOOK GROUPS: FINDING YOUR PEOPLE

Joining a Facebook Group that aligns with your business is a valuable way to build awareness, and support your customers. However, to use Groups effectively, you must understand that Facebook did not create the Group feature for brand promotion. Your Facebook Page plays that role. But you can get business value from joining Groups and potentially creating one yourself.

Next, read about the top three things to keep in mind for your business to get the most value from Groups:

- Groups are for users, not businesses.
- Do not market to Groups, but be very helpful.
- Use Groups for team communications.

GROUPS ARE FOR USERS, NOT BUSINESSES

In the earlier days of Facebook, businesses would create Facebook Groups in which customers or clients can join to receive updates, offers, and information. Now a business's Facebook Page serves those functions. This functionality move allowed Groups to become spaces that form organically from a groundswell of Facebook's network of users. Only users (and not businesses) can add one another to Groups in order to form communities based on interests, jobs, politics, and other commonalities, including relationships, such as family and close friends.

Since only friends can invite other friends to a Group, that poses a very high barrier to adoption, so the practice of creating one around your business becomes impractical. Creating a Group for your business also may not be a wise move because it can backfire and cause damage to how people perceive your brand. If Groups are meant to be organic, and thus authentic, anything commercial in nature would be perceived as intrusive and disingenuous.

Bottom line: Avoid creating a Group for your business for the purpose of attracting customers.

DO NOT MARKET TO GROUPS, BUT BE VERY HELPFUL

Requesting to join a Group whose users have interests that align with your product or service is a very effective way of finding prospective customers. If you are admitted to the Group, you will be permitted to write posts to the Group's News Feed. This is where you will have the power to publicize yourself, but you must be responsible with this power. If you post blatant promotions that show no care for the theme of the Group and you do this often, you will be seen as a spammer. If people want to receive your business's updates and promotions, they will like your Facebook Page. Not everyone in the Groups that you join has done that, so do not treat all Group members like your fans. Otherwise you will turn them into your detractors.

Instead, focus on providing a public service and being informative by asking and answering questions as a way to engage with the other members of the Group. This is how you create connections with people that form into relationships, people who have the potential to become customers, referrals, or business partners.

One way of providing service that aligns with a Group's interests is by promoting an event that your business will be hosting. Post notifications about the event to the Group's News Feed; just do not be sales-y about it.

The most effective way to promote your business is really by promoting yourself as a caring, thoughtful, informed, and insightful community member of the Group. It is the Group equivalent of thought-leadership articles that businesses publish in industry publications and the blog section of their websites. This activity, performed in a manner with no strings attached, will go a long way toward building your brand.

USE GROUPS FOR TEAM COMMUNICATIONS

For businesses that have a fairly significant number of team members, the biggest opportunity for them to use Groups is by creating a community inside the company to foster communication. You can add your company's employees and partners to a private Group, thus using it as a free alternative to internal, corporate, social media platforms like Yammer.

Team members can share updates on what they are working on and links to information that would be helpful to the organization. You also can use Groups to make company announcements.

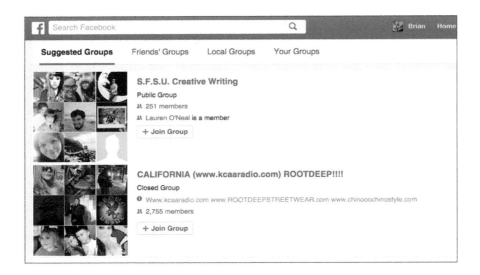

FIGURE 7

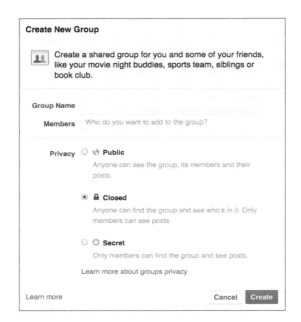

FIGURE 8

JOINING FACEBOOK GROUPS

Here's how to sign up for a Facebook Group:

1. *Click Groups on the left side of your Facebook Page.* You will see the Suggested Groups feature, which is a good way to find Groups that align with your business.

2. *Once you find Groups that seem to have community members who would be interested in your business, read their descriptions to identify those accepting new members.* Then request to join the Group by clicking Join in the top-right corner of the Group's page.

SETTING UP YOUR OWN INTERNAL GROUP

Follow these steps to create your own internal group:

1. *Go to your Groups page and click the button Create Group.* A pop-up screen appears in which you can name your Group, add members, and set your Group's privacy.

   Once you have named your Group, you must add at least one person to the group. This person should be a team member of your business.

2. *Set your Group's privacy.* There are three privacy settings: Public, Closed, and Secret. Select the Closed Group setting for your business group.

3. *Select an icon that will appear beside your Group's name in the Groups list.*

4. *Manage the settings by clicking the ellipsis icon (three dots) on the right-hand side under the header and selecting Edit Group Settings.* This will bring up the Edit Group Settings pop-up window. Here you can define membership settings and add a description.

   To customize your Group's URL, click the Setup Group Email button to open the Create Group Email Address window. Type the URL for your Facebook group in the space provided. Click OK when you are done changing the URL.

Personalize Your Group

Did you know that you can add a photo here?
Pick one that shows off your group's personality.

Upload Photo   Choose Photo ▾

Fiction Advocates
Secret Group

Joined ▾   Message   ✓ Notifications   •••

Discussion   Members   Events   Photos   Files   Search this group

Group Name   ⬚ ▾ Fiction Advocates

Privacy   ○ 🌐 **Public**
Anyone can see the group, its members and their posts.

○ 🔒 **Closed**
Anyone can find the group and see who's in it. Only members can see posts.

◉ ⊘ **Secret**
Only members can find the group and see posts.

Membership Approval   ◉ Any member can add or approve members.
○ Any member can add members, but an admin must approve them.

Web and Email Address   Customize your group's contact info, so you can quickly share a link to your group or email all your members.
Customize Address

Description
Potential members see the description if privacy is set to public or closed.

FIGURE 9

Posting Permissions	◉ Members and admins can post to the group. ○ Only admins can post to the group.
Post Approval	☐ All group posts must be approved by an admin.

FIGURE 10

5. *Create tags for your Group. Set posting permissions and approvals.*

6. *Define your Group settings for permissions and approvals.* You now have the ability to add people automatically to your Group if they are in your network. Or, you can use your Group's URL in a message or e-mail to invite people to join your Group.

FACEBOOK INSIGHTS FOR ORGANIC TRAFFIC

One of the biggest benefits of having a Facebook Page versus merely a personal profile is that you have free access to Facebook Insights. As an SMB owner, research plays a pivotal role in the decisions you make about your marketing. Facebook Insights lets you analyze how your Facebook audience has been responding to the tactics that you have employed on your Facebook Page. You can see what people have clicked on and the times of day when they are most active.

ACCESSING FACEBOOK INSIGHTS

Here's how to access Facebook Insights:

1. Find the Insights button in the middle of the Admin Panel at the top of your Facebook Page.

2. Click it to view your performance metrics. This view acts as your metrics dashboard.

3. Click each tab above your graph to dive into each of the metrics shown across the top. You will get a detailed view into the behavior of your audience and the content in which they have shown interest.

4. Scroll down below the graph to see a list of your posts and their associated metrics segmented into columns named Date, Post, Reach, Engaged Users, Talking About This, and Virality.

Following is a description of each metric. For all of you Excel jockeys out there, note that you can export this data to a file by clicking the Table icon, so you can dive even deeper into the data.

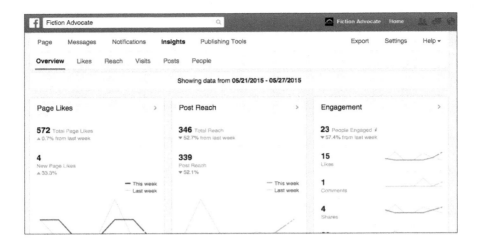

FIGURE 11

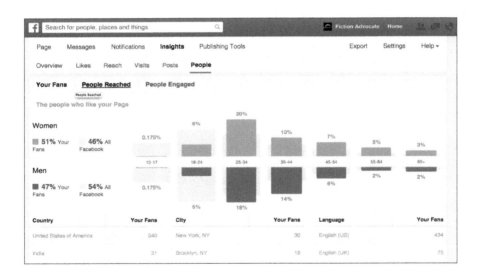

FIGURE 12

Date

This column displays the date that you created the post.

Post

The icon located to the left of each listed post indicates whether your post contained an image, a link, or only text. Sorting the list by each of the metrics—Reach, Engaged Users, Talking About This, or Virality—is how you find patterns.

Industry pundits have commented on Facebook's predilection to show a specific type of content to more of your audience. So if you sort by Reach (which represents the size of an audience), you might discover that more text-only posts filter to the top. In this example, the insight would be that more people have seen your text-only posts than your other content. If you had not analyzed the performance of your posts through Facebook Insights, you would never have known that you could reach a larger audience through posts without images or links. This is a classic example of identifying how to game the system by analyzing the data freely available to you.

Reach

Reach is defined, in Facebook terms, as the number of unique people who have seen your post. Facebook's EdgeRank algorithm decides the percentage of your audience that you can reach. The Reach metric shows you how many people saw your post. If you analyze the table sorting by this metric, you can see the type of posts that received the highest reach.

Engaged Users

The Engaged Users metric tracks the number of unique people who clicked your post. This metric has nothing to do with other actions that people might have taken on your post, such as comments, likes, and shares, which is normally how people think about engagement. This metric allows you to track and analyze the performance of your posts that contained links, which are the only clickable things you can include in a post. Think of this metric as akin to click-through rate (CTR) for search.

Talking About This

This is the engagement metric. However, Facebook defines it like this: the number of unique people who have created a story from your Page post. In Facebook terminology, *stories* are likes, comments on, or shares of your post; answers to a question that you posted; or responses to one of your events. You can use this metric to determine the types of content that compel your audience into conversational actions, that is, beyond clicks. Usually you will find that posts with a high–Talking About This ratio reached only a low percentage of your audience.

Recall that text-only posts usually generate high-Reach ratios. Now you know that posts with richer content are more likely to generate stories. With this data, you can use the purchase funnel to make informed decisions about your content mix based on which metric you want to drive:

Awareness: Text-only to attain the highest reach

Consideration: Rich content to start and keep the conversation going

Transaction: Links to take people to your website or e-commerce store to make purchases

Loyalty and Advocacy: A mix of links to exclusive deals for existing customers and rich content for them to share with friends.

Virality

This is the most complex metric in the table. Its formula is Talking About This divided by Reach. In other words, it is the percentage calculated from the number of people who liked, commented on, or shared your post against the number of people who have seen your post. You can think of this metric as your conversation rate—it is a measurement of the percentage of your audience that found your content compelling.

INSTAGRAM: MARKETING TO THE NEW TREEHOUSE

Instagram is a free social media platform for all to use. It connects consumers to brands globally every day. As an SMB owner who must manage your resources tightly, whether that be labor or direct costs, you need to spend your time and money efficiently. So you should ask yourself whether leveraging yet another marketing channel is right for your business.

IS INSTAGRAM RIGHT FOR YOU?

Facebook started out life on the desktop computer as a college treehouse free from the prying eyes of adults. But as it got bigger and bigger, the adults moved in. This naturally caused the kids to find other treehouses to which they could escape their parents getting updates about their so-called secret lives in their News Feeds. And ever since the iPhone was introduced into our daily lives, the traffic coming into Facebook from mobile devices has grown steadily to now comprising more than half of the total amount of traffic. Soon the majority of Facebook traffic will be mobile.

So where have the "kids" gone? As the saying goes, the apple does not fall far from the tree: They have moved to Instagram, which Facebook acquired in 2012 and is the centerpiece of the company's mobile-app ecosystem. According to Pew Research, more than half of the Internet population between the ages of 18 and 29 use Instagram. Half of them use it daily.

If your target audience includes millennials, then the answer to whether or not you should do Instagram marketing to support your Facebook marketing is a resounding YES.

If not, then allocate your resources to bolstering other marketing channels that will support your Facebook marketing.

HOW TO SET UP AN INSTAGRAM BUSINESS PAGE

The Instagram interface contains the options that are described next.

Profile Picture

The size of your Profile Picture is limited to 150 by 150 pixels. Instagram automatically will crop it into a circle, so be sure to use a photo that shows up well in a circle. To add your Profile Picture, tap the photo circle. The following options will appear:

- Import profile photo from Facebook.
- Import profile photo from Twitter.
- Take your own photo, a.k.a., selfie.
- Choose photo from library.

Because this is your Instagram business page, be sure to choose an image that represents your brand, products, or services.

Instagram Settings (a.k.a. The Gear)

Here are explanations of these options:

Follow People: Use this feature to follow people and businesses on Instagram and to invite people to follow your profile.

- Find Facebook Friends.
- Find Contacts: Sync Instagram with your contacts list.
- Invite Friends.

Account: Here you can edit your profile, change your password, see the photos that you have liked, and set your profile to private or public. As a business, your profile should be public.

Other Settings: Here you can link, or later unlink, your profile to other social media profiles, define notification settings, save original photos, or preload videos with Wi-Fi only or using cellular data as well.

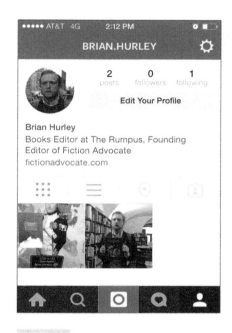

FIGURE 13

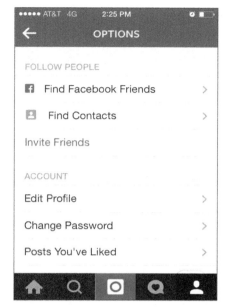

FIGURE 14

@username

This is where you enter the name of your profile. You can use your own name or company name. Since this is your business profile, the best practice is to use your company name. Also, the name you choose becomes your Instagram URL, e.g., www.instagram.com/[yourinstagram_username].

Posts

The number that shows up here is the amount of images you have posted. Tapping it invokes your image gallery.

Followers

The number that shows up here is the amount of followers that you have amassed. Tapping this brings up a list of all the people who are following your account.

Following

The number that shows up here is the amount of people you are following. A good way of identifying prospective customers is to follow your competitors to see the people they are following.

Edit Profile

This section is as important for you to complete as was the About section on your Facebook Page. You are limited to 150 characters in this section. Since the space given to you here is much smaller than that on Facebook, treat it as a tweet and write about the value that your business provides.

Image Galleries

This is where you choose how you prefer to view images in the gallery—either tiled or in one column. Image-view options include two choices: (1) as a tiled gallery or (2) in one column, one at a time.

Location

This feature allows you to add location data to the photos that you post. Adding geographic tags to photos allows them to show up on maps. This is a valuable marketing tool for local businesses with physical locations or defined service areas.

Tagged Images

This feature allows you to find images in which your business appeared and was tagged. For example, a customer could have taken a photo of themselves using your product or standing near your store.

Gallery

This part of the screen is where you can view your collection of images. Tapping an image brings it into full view and displays information about people who liked it or commented on it.

Home

This icon takes you to your News Feed, which comprises a gallery of images that the people you are following have posted.

Search

The search feature allows you to search through Instagram in two ways:

- **Users and Hashtags:** This option allows you to search for specific users or hashtags.
- **Photos and People:** This option allows you to let Instagram recommend photos and people based on your preferences and activities.

Instagram Icon

Tapping this icon invokes a screen containing the following functions:

1. Close the screen by tapping X.
2. Invoke the Rule of Thirds feature that professional photographers use.
3. Take a selfie and post it to Instagram.
4. Post photos or videos from your device's photo library.
5. Camera shutter: Tap it to take a photo within Instagram
6. Video recorder: Tap it to start shooting a video within Instagram.

Notifications

Functioning similarly to the Activity feature of your Facebook Page, this feature shows you who liked your photos or provided a comment and who is following you.

Back to Profile

This icon takes you back to your profile when you are in a different screen.

TEN WAYS TO WIELD INSTAGRAM POWERFULLY

Setting up your Instagram profile and learning your way around the app is the easy part. You want to get the most out of your Instagram presence and turn it into a powerful marketing channel that helps drive your Facebook marketing strategy. So, here are 10 ways to optimize and maintain your Instagram profile so that it piques the interest of potential consumers and keeps your current customers interested.

1. *Add a link to your website/Facebook Page in the Bio section.* Doing this not only allows people to connect to you outside of Instagram, but also drives leads to your website.

2. *Learn how to take better photos on your smartphone.* As an SMB, investing in an expensive DSLR (digital single-lens reflex) camera to take high-quality photos most likely does not fit into your budget. If you have a newer smartphone model, the built-in camera has all the power you will need to take compelling photos. Here are some tips:

   - *Crop, don't zoom.* Image quality noticeably degrades when using the zoom function, so crop your images if you want to use just part of them.

   - *Edit, don't filter.* If you want unique images to remain unique, then edit them instead of using the same filters that everyone else on Instagram is using.

   - *Use a better camera app.* This is applicable more to iPhone than Android users, but the goal is the same: more camera control than the built-in camera app gives you.

   - *Don't use the flash.* Smartphone flashes do not actually flash or strobe, so color gets washed out; in low light, find a different light source.

   - *Clean the lens.* Seems simple, but we handle our phones all day and keep them in dirty pockets or bags.

3. ***Tell a story.*** Stories drive interest and interaction, in real life and on Instagram. So rather than posting one-off photos, create a story by sharing a series of photos that illustrate associated actions progressing over time.

Instagram started out as an app for sharing photos, but you also can share video clips on it. However, do not use it for long videos. The best approach to using Instagram for videos is to reuse the ones you have uploaded to your website and Facebook Page, but select only a 15-second clip from them.

4. ***Add text to your photos.*** *Memes* are images that contain a combination of graphics and text. Just as these images are more likely to go viral on the Internet, they tend to get more traction on Instagram. So take advantage of this phenomenon by creating your own graphic and text combinations.

5. ***Do not sell; tell your story instead.*** You should approach marketing your brand on Instagram with the same indirectness as building awareness of your business in Facebook Groups. Think of it as creating thought leadership that educates and informs people about your industry. No one likes overpromotion. It turns people off. So the content you upload should be about supporting the organic community that you are building on the foundation of your Instagram profile.

6. ***Give "exclusive" insights into your business.*** This suggestion both conflicts with and supports the earlier suggestion of posting high-quality photos. Showing candid and unpolished photos of what is happening at your business personalizes your brand in a down-to-earth way. Introducing your team members and new employees is good way to do this.

7. ***Highlight new uses and new products.*** Sometimes your followers want you to be direct. Showing them new ways to use your products gives your followers something valuable in exchange for their time. It also increases the value of the product for customers who have already purchased it.

Similarly, previewing new products before they are released to the general public gives these products an aura of exclusivity. For some people, this is a fair value exchange for their attention.

8. **Use relevant hashtags.** Hashtags are words and phrases that identify messages on a particular topic. They're preceded by a hash or pound (#) sign. Use them to identify photos, videos, and messages on a specific topic. You can use certain hashtags to reach the audience you want through the hashtag categories that your customers and potential partners are using.

   Using the right hashtags for your photos is vitally important. Doing this can allow your content to ride the wave of other material that has gained traction. This way, your content has a better chance of showing up in searches. Before posting anything, search for similar content to understand the types of hashtags that can help your material gain awareness and engagement.

9. **Distribute your Instagram content to Facebook and Twitter.** Do not forget about posting your Instagram links to your Facebook Page and Twitter (if you are using it). Doing this will help create a virtuous cycle that grows your follower and fan bases across the social networks on which you have a presence.

10. **Figure out when and how often to post.** Once you start posting content in earnest, pay attention to the time of day your posts receive the highest number of likes and comments. Analyze these trends and use these insights to identify the optimal times of day when your audience is most receptive.

    Equally, be aware of your *feed speed*. This is the principle of too much of a good thing turning bad. Do not overload your audience with content and turn them off. You can discern your feed speed by tracking the posting frequency of successful brands in your industry that are similar in size to your business.

SUCCESS STORY

Instagram Marketing
in Action

ADVERTISER PROFILE
NAME: LikaLove
TYPE OF BUSINESS: Independent women's clothing boutique
MONTHLY FACEBOOK AD SPEND: $0.00 (all organic traffic)

LikaLove is a women's clothing boutique that started out life as
a mobile fashion truck. Owner Malika Siddiq is a Seattle native
whose philosophy is that "fashion is worth being passionate
about, and style is a way to say who you are without having
to speak."

Malika is passionate about marketing her brand through social media.
Of course, she started on Facebook. And why not when she considered her
target market? Women of all shapes, sizes, and styles who want to be comfortable, feel sexy, and have something new to show off are on Facebook.

Malika decided to open a brick-and-mortar store. She wanted to increase
traffic to her store while continuing to build the cool and funky brand of her
mobile boutique. She had heard of food trucks that used Twitter to tell people
where they were going to be parked. This seemed like a natural strategy to use
with her mobile boutique. She also saw that many of her customers used
Instagram to upload photos of themselves wearing the clothing that they had
bought from her mobile fashion truck. So, she wanted to leverage the marketing
that her customers already were doing on her behalf by engaging with them on
the Facebook-owned app.

FIGURE 15

FIND YOUR PEOPLE AND PLAY WHERE THEY PLAY: Malika uses Instagram to engage with her current and potential customers. She does this by posting photos of herself, friends, and employees wearing the trending brands in her inventory. Whether it is a photo of an employee wearing a new dress, a happy customer wearing a new outfit for a night out, or a freshly stocked rack of new items, she posts all of these to Instagram. That's where they catch the attention of her current shoppers and their friends when the photos are shared.

Malika also uses the GPS location feature on Instagram to let shoppers know where she is when selling from her fashion truck. In parallel, she will send a tweet about her location, which also shows up on her Facebook Page, as she has her two accounts linked. Integrating the latest technology available through the social media channels that she uses is an absolute must for driving brand awareness and revenue.

PICK EFFECTIVE HASHTAGS: Hashtags are an effective method of connecting consumers to brands globally. Malika uses the hashtag #Seattle in many of her posts. Doing so generates likes from consumers who either use the same hashtag or scroll through the page for that hashtag. This is a free and easy way to connect with her local target market and raise brand awareness.

THINK GLOBALLY, ACT LOCALLY: Major retailers know the power of Instagram. They run campaigns like "Last of your favorites" or "Final Farewell" to promote sale items and discontinued merchandise and to attract shoppers that are more likely to engage in the post. Even though LikaLove is still a business and has nowhere near the operating budget of the major retailers, Malika is able to compete with them effectively on Instagram because she approaches her marketing with the same savvy.

When small businesses are devising the content and messaging to target their markets, Malika's advice is to ask, who am I trying to reach, engage, or get to like my brand, and why? She says that you need to allocate the time for testing to identify what content and messages are working. Malika also recommends that you conceptualize why and how to improve the material to reach a broader audience. Once you have done that, be confident in your decision.

LikaLove employed three specific Instagram strategies that continue to be successful. The tactics that comprise these strategies can be applied to any retail business, regardless of size. It just so happens that they work; LikaLove is a (successful) small business.

- Run social media promotional campaigns.
- Receive a percentage off your purchase.
- Take advantage of Instagram or Facebook exclusive specials (for example, "Mention this post and receive $10 off any purchase of $50 or more").

- Feature sale items.
- Engage with customers.
- Create posts that promote interaction between your brand and customers; e.g., upload two new pieces of inventory (like dresses) and ask people to comment on which one they like best.
- Respond to all inquiries sent through social media to show your appreciation.
- Be flexible. Offer shipping when needed and different sizes or styles if they are not readily available.
- Make sure your customer always feels valued.
- Hold special events.
- Be a part of your community. Promote other SMBs and give each other recognition through social media.
- Host private or exclusive events if possible. LikaLove offers private shopping parties where customers can book the fashion truck for their own private events.
- Participate in fundraisers for a charity of your choice. Do this at least once a year, as it is a great way to generate brand awareness for your business, while giving back (a win-win). Any expenses associated with fundraising can be a tax deduction, too.

USING TWITTER TO SUPPORT FACEBOOK

Many small businesses started their digital marketing efforts on Twitter. In some ways, it is easier to start on Twitter than on Facebook. If you don't have a Twitter account, set one up because some of your current and potential customers use it more often than they use Facebook. Furthermore, the ability to cross-reference your posts between Facebook and Twitter means that your messages will reach both audiences who use one more often than the other. People who use both social media networks will be exposed to your messages more often without feeling as if they are being inundated.

There are two ways to repurpose your Facebook and Twitter posts:

1. Have your Facebook posts distributed as tweets automatically.

2. Automatically post your tweets and retweets to your Facebook Wall.

HOW TO LINK YOUR FACEBOOK PAGE TO TWITTER

Follow these steps to link your Facebook account to Twitter:

1. ***Log in to the Twitter application on Facebook:*** Apps.facebook.com/twitter.

2. ***Click the Sign in with Twitter button under Connect Your Accounts.*** Now your personal Facebook Page is linked to your Twitter account. This is a necessary step before you can link your business Facebook Page to your Twitter account.

3. ***Go to Facebook.com/twitter.*** On this page, you will be able to link all of your Facebook pages, including your business page, to Twitter.

4. ***Click the Link to Twitter button.*** You will be redirected to a Twitter login page.

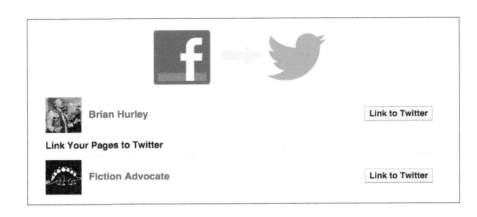

FIGURE 16

FIGURE 17

5. **Sign in to your Twitter account to confirm the link between the two accounts.** Type your Twitter username and password and click Allow. You then will be redirected back to your Facebook account.

6. **Select which content to post to Twitter.** In Edit Settings, decide which content you want to share with Twitter:

   - Status updates
   - Links
   - Photos
   - Notes
   - Events

7. **Click Save Changes.** Now you can post a status update in Facebook. It will be sent as a Facebook link to your Twitter page, where a status update will be posted for you automatically. Remember to limit your posts to 137 characters, which leaves space for the characters "RT" (ReTweet).

HOW TO ADD A TWITTER FEED TO YOUR FACEBOOK PAGE

Follow these instructions to accomplish this task:

1. **Log into the Twitter account that you use for your business.**

2. **Go to the Settings menu's Apps tab.**

3. **Click Connect to Facebook.** If you have not logged into your Facebook account yet, the Facebook login prompt will appear.

4. **Type your login credentials and click Log In.** A prompt will appear that stating that Twitter will receive certain information from your Facebook account.

5. **Click OK.** Another prompt will appear for you to select the privacy settings regarding whom you want to see your Tweets and Retweets on your Facebook Wall—it is set to Friends by default.

6. **Click OK.**

FACEBOOK ADS: ARE THEY RIGHT FOR YOU?

So far this book has shown you how to generate organic traffic to your Facebook Page by creating a symbiotic relationship among your other digital marketing channels. The goal has been to drive organic traffic across all of the channels. Whether you are a small business, a multimillion dollar company, or a massive global brand, generating organic traffic is the ultimate goal of your advertising strategy.

As an SMB owner, the first and most important part of your digital marketing mission is to optimize your Facebook Page, website, and other Web presences so that they are in the best possible positions to receive and generate organic traffic. If you have gotten this far, you are well on your way to Facebook marketing success.

But what about spending money on Facebook Ads? As you are very likely a Facebook user yourself, you see these ads on your own Facebook Page. Of course, all the large companies seem to be doing it, and smaller companies seem to be doing it as well.

This begs the question . . . are Facebook Ads worth it for you?

The answer is, they can be if you approach them with the same thoughtfulness and care as you have with your organic marketing and use them as supporting mechanisms to produce more organic traffic.

TARGETING PRECISION

Facebook Ads offer as many or more options and data for targeting customers than any other digital marketing channel. You can target almost any niche and subniche that you can imagine. Not just that, you can add targeting dimensions like where your niche lives and what time of day the ads should be shown to them.

One of the strongest uses for Facebook Ads is to compel people in very specific demographic and psychographic segments to like your Facebook Page. This approach allows you to nurture a relationship with them over time. For example, local businesses can get people within their area to like their page. This is similar to building an e-mail list but with a much lower barrier for the user. Then the local businesses can give their new fans coupons or promote events on their Facebook Pages. They can include incentives for their fans to share those promotions with their friends, and all of a sudden you get viral advertising from a few well-placed and well-timed Facebook Ads.

BETTER THAN E-MAIL

Using Facebook Ads to get people to like your Facebook Page is similar to building an e-mail list. There are inherently fewer reservations for the user, and the ads are much cheaper than sending direct mail marketing. Facebook Ads also provide significantly higher levels of control and data. As an SMB owner, you can create a growing community of potential customers that will be around possibly for years.

LESS COMPETITIVE AND MORE COMFORTABLE THAN SEARCH

The competition for PPC (pay-per-click) keywords is much lower on Facebook Ads than on major search engines. Furthermore, Facebook users see your ads on their Facebook Pages rather than on an impersonal search-results page. You are reaching your consumers in their comfort zone. When they see your ad on their profile, there is a built-in level of trust that they would not experience when seeing a random link on a search-results page.

Think about it this way—the people seeing your Facebook Ad can go to your Facebook Page, whereas clicking a search link takes them to your website. The biggest difference between a Facebook Page and a website is the presence of customer feedback. So when people click your Facebook Ad and are redirected to your Facebook Page, they can read what other people are saying about your business. This has the effect of building trust with consumers in a way that your website can never do.

EMPOWERING FACEBOOK ADS

Now that you have a better handle on how to wield Facebook Ads, it is worthwhile at this point to get a deeper understanding of where you as an SMB fit in the Facebook Ad environment. You should be aware of how different types of Facebook Ads work, the features that are available to SMBs as opposed to large companies, and how these features are made available to different types of advertisers. This knowledge will empower you to get the most out of the money you decide to spend on Facebook Ads.

THE FACEBOOK SALES PROCESS

There are three channels through which Facebook sells ads to advertisers:

1. *Direct Sales:* This team provides personalized services to the largest global brands, managing these million-dollar relationships directly with the advertisers themselves and also through their agencies. Facebook's Premium product is available only to major accounts.

2. *Inside Sales:* This team manages the subsequent level of advertisers, with budgets in the upper-hundred thousands of dollars. Their budgets are not as large as the upper tier but still significant enough to warrant a sales representative managing a portfolio of these types of accounts.

3. *Self-serve:* As an SMB, your business fits into this category. This means that you will buy Facebook Ads through the self-serve website. But that's okay, because you have this book to walk you through the process.

MARKETPLACE ADS

Marketplace Ads are desktop advertisements that appear on a person's Facebook profile sidebar. These ads include a headline, body copy, and an image. Clicking these types of ads leads to a Facebook Page or an app on Facebook, as well as to a business website.

Marketplace Ads are designed to be more engaging than traditional display ads. They are more of a one-way communication. This is in comparison to Sponsored Stories, which are meant to inspire a two-way conversation that allows viewers to like, comment, and share the ad.

There are four types of Marketplace Ads:

1. *Standard Ad:* for website traffic
2. *Like Ad:* for Facebook-profile traffic
3. *App Ad:* for app traffic
4. *Event Ad:* for event promotions

Although video ads are offered to large advertisers, they are not available through the self-serve channel. However, videos are available to self-serve advertisers through Page Post Ads, which are described on page 74.

SPONSORED STORIES

Sponsored Stories revolve around user activity. When you elect to buy these ads, you pay to highlight actions that users already have performed on Facebook itself or on a Facebook-connected app. These actions show up in the Facebook Page sidebar or the News Feed of the friends of the users who performed the highlighted actions. In this way, Sponsored Stories are designed to be more trustworthy than Marketplace Ads. They reach only the friends of the people who have performed an action on your Facebook Page.

Unlike Marketplace Ads, you do not have creative control over these ad types because users are creating them through their natural actions. These ad types also are referred to as "voice of friend," that is, ads generated by your fans and shown to their friends when they interact with your brand. The fan's Profile Picture and name show up in these ads, which distinguish them from Marketplace Ads by adding a social dimension.

The following fan actions generate Sponsored Stories:

- *Page Like:* fan likes your page
- *Page Post Like:* fan likes your post
- *Page Post Comment:* fan comments on your post
- *App Used or App Shared:* fan uses or shares your app
- *Check In:* fan checks in to your location
- *Question Answered:* fan answers a question that you posted
- *Event RSVP:* fan will attend your event

The goal of Sponsored Stories is to inspire more people to take the same action that their friends have taken. For example, if you want more people to like your Facebook Page, you can buy a Page Like Sponsored Story.

PAGE POST ADS

Page Post Ads start out as posts on your Facebook Page. They get further paid distribution among your fans and their friends, and to people not yet connected to your Facebook Page through a friend. These types of ads give you the power to show content on your Facebook Page in an ad unit on the sidebar of a person's Facebook profile, as well as in his or her News Feed.

Page Post Ad types include the following:

• Text posts

• Photo posts

• Video posts

• Link posts

• Questions/Polls that you've posted

• Event posts

You should leverage Page Post Ads as part of your content-marketing strategy, as well as promoting events and offers. But for acquiring fans, stick with Marketplace Ads and Sponsored Stories.

Accounts with larger budgets have access to Facebook Premium. This feature is a Page Post Ad that allows fans to like or add a comment directly in the ad. Self-serve advertisers do not get this option.

FACEBOOK OFFERS

These ads allow you to create an offer that can be posted on your Facebook Page, which your fans can claim with one click. Your fans' friends will see that they claimed your offer in their News Feeds and be prompted to claim it as well. Facebook Offers work a little differently from the other Facebook Ads. You can set Offers up directly from your Facebook Page, meaning there is no need to go to the Facebook Ads dashboard.

You can hypertarget your Offers so that only your fans and their friends who would most likely be interested in them will see them. When people click your Offer, Facebook sends an e-mail to their personal e-mail accounts. When these people open the e-mail containing your Offer, they will see a link to your website or an opt-in page based on where you want them to claim your Offer.

THE AD LOGIC OF THE NEWS FEED

Big advertisers have access to a feature called Promoted Posts, which get inserted directly into the News Feeds of their fans. Although as a self-serve advertiser you do not get this feature, your Sponsored Stories and Page Posts show up in News Feeds based on the relevance score that the EdgeRank gives them.

EdgeRank gathers data on how your ads perform when they are placed in News Feeds and on mobile devices. This practice optimizes both the user experience and the effectiveness of your ads. If your ad shows up in a person's News Feed, you will pay for impressions CPM (cost per mille) or CPC (cost per click), just as you would for a Marketplace Ad. The different ways that the costs of ads are calculated are explained later in Allocating Ad Spend for Small Budgets on page 80.

FACEBOOK AUDIENCE INSIGHTS: RECOGNIZING YOUR POTENTIAL PARTNERS

Even if you applied all the best practices that you have learned from this book into creating a great and comprehensive ad for your business, the ad still can fail. That is, it did not reach the audience for which you had created the ad in the first place. Rather than gambling your ad budget, you can spend it wisely by learning about the people whom your ad will reach. You can do this with Facebook Audience Insights, which is a separate tool from Facebook Insights.

Although both Power Editor and Ad Creation allow you to customize your campaign's target audience, these tools do not provide deeper audience insights before you launch your campaign. Audience Insights lets you learn about specific audience segments before putting your ad budget on the line.

SELF-REPORTED AND OFF-FACEBOOK SOURCES

Audience Insights combines data from two main sources:

Self-Reported: This is data that people enter to build and maintain their personal profiles, including age, gender, likes, relationship status, jobs, and education level.

Off-Facebook: This data is provided by third-party companies, called data brokers, and includes data such as purchasing behavior, home market value, and household income. As this data is inferred rather than directly entered, it does not come even close to Facebook's data in terms of accuracy.

USING AUDIENCE INSIGHTS

Follow these instructions to use Audience Insights:

Choose or create an audience. These are your options:

- Everyone on Facebook
- People connected to your page
- A custom audience

You also can use the sidebar to create a custom audience, which includes the same segmenting options available on Power Editor and Ad Creation:

- Custom audience—uses an existing custom audience
- Location
- Age and gender
- Interests
- Connections—allows for the inclusion or exclusion of your fans
- Advanced—lets you filter based on behaviors, language, relationship status, education, work, finances, home, market segments, parents, politics, life events, and devices

Survey the data to define your audience. The data is segmented into six tabs:

Demographics

- Age and Gender: Information from Facebook profiles of users 18 and older
- Lifestyle: US demographic and interest data based on purchase behavior, brand affinity, and other activities
- Relationship Status: Information from Facebook profiles of users 18 and older about their relationship status
- Education Level: Information from Facebook profiles of users 18 and older about their highest levels of education
- Job Title: Information from Facebook profiles of users 18 and older about the industries in which they work

Page Likes The Page Likes tab has two sets of affinity-focused data:

- Top Categories: This data is based on the interests that Facebook users liked divided into categories
- Page Likes: A list of Facebook Pages deemed to be what your audience segment has liked

Location Use this tab to identify users who live in geographic areas that you want to target:

- Top cities
- Top countries
- Top languages

Activity This data is useful in targeting the type of people who are most likely to perform the action that your ad requires and for deciding on which device you should show your ad.

- Frequency of Activities: The number of times your audience performed certain activities such as liking, sharing, commenting, redeeming promotions, and clicking ads
- Device Users: Provides a summary of the devices that your audience used to log into Facebook over the last 30 days

Household Available only for Facebook users in the United States, this data is based on survey responses, purchase activity, and census and publicly available data from third-party data brokers; beware that the accuracy of this data is much lower than Facebook's self-reported data.

- Household income
- Home ownership
- Household size
- Home market value
- Spending methods

Purchase More third-party data, this tab offers information on the purchasing behavior of US households.

- Retail spending
- Online purchases
- Purchase behavior
- Vehicle research

Click each tab to bring up its chart and adjust the characteristics of audience segments from the sidebar. By default, the data is sorted based on *affinity*, which means the likelihood of a segment being in this audience is compared with the average Facebook user.

Save your defined audience. Click the Save menu item from the top menu. Give your new audience a name and click Save. Your new audience will be available to you in Power Editor under Saved Groups, or you can use it and continue to create an ad.

Click Create an Ad on the top-right corner of the screen. A pop-up window will appear, allowing you to use Create Ad or Power Editor.

Advanced Analysis

Wielding the power of Audience Insights requires a deeper understanding of its unique features. Unless you are aware of the nuances of how the data is reported, your analysis will be misinformed, which might lead you to incorrect conclusions. Here are a few tips on getting a handle on the data.

The Median Is Not the Average The data shown in the Frequency of Activities chart shows the median, not the average. The *median* is the halfway point between the higher half of the data and the lower half. The reason median can be a more accurate way to represent a collection of data is that it is not affected by outliers, the extreme values that can move the average of the data set away from the median.

Facebook is a vast digital community representing actual people and entities. So, the data that is generated by its population behaves similarly to real-world communities. Behaviors outside the norm stem from spam accounts, promotion hunters, or regular people following temporary trends. Facebook's use of the median calculates extreme behavior out of the data, so that way you do not target the extremities.

Connections Are Different from Interests The Interests area in the left sidebar is an effective way to carry out competitive research. You can type the name of brands or businesses like yours and get audience data on those Facebook Pages. But the report does not characterize the fans of those Pages—it signifies the people who have expressed an interest in the terms on which you searched, including but not limited to those Pages' fans.

Here are a few variables to consider when analyzing Interests:

- Data includes fans who have not interacted with those Pages in quite a while, so it is highly likely that you will not reach them.
- People who have shared, liked, or commented on content within those Pages but have not liked the Page itself will be present in that audience.
- People who have used the keywords that you used to search in their posts may be represented in that audience.

You can use the Connections area to limit the audience to fans, but here you can include only your own Facebook Page.

"All Facebook" Means Your Countries On the reports that you generate, Facebook Audience Insights compares the data for the audience that you created to "All Facebook." One would think that means the entire Facebook population. In fact, this data represents the countries that you selected when creating your audience.

Equally, if you started creating your audience by choosing cities, states, or regions rather than countries, the "All Facebook" data rolls up automatically to the countries in which those areas are located.

Lifetime vs. Last 30 Days

The Frequency of Activities report in the Activity menu shows two separate time frames:

1. Lifetime data for the "Pages Liked" chart
2. Last 30 days data for all the other metrics

Most people like Pages far less often than they like or comment on a post. As a result, data for the Pages that an audience liked is much more stable than that for all the other activities people perform on Facebook. So, you can draw accurate conclusions from the lifetime data for Pages Liked. The last 30 days makes more sense for the remaining metrics. Those activities represent notions and affinities that are more temporal than actually becoming a fan of a Page.

ALLOCATING AD SPEND FOR SMALL BUDGETS

By this point in the book, you know how to create a compelling ad and finely target it to your niche market. As an SMB owner, you cannot just throw money at your advertising in the hopes of making it work. It would be nice to know how much you will need to spend to get the return from your ad campaigns that you hope to receive.

There is no easy way to pinpoint this solution. Only you can eventually figure out how to allocate your budget optimally, whether you are spending hundreds or thousands per month. It will come down to trial and error on the way to success. Having said that, there are some rules of thumb that you should consider in terms of budget allocation. There are also rough industry estimates for ad costs at your disposal.

Again, bear in mind that all costs quoted here are approximations. Facebook is an auction, and prices vary on a daily basis.

MAXIMUM AND MINIMUM SPENDS

You can set your maximum dollar budget per day or maximum dollar budget for the lifetime of a campaign, but you cannot have both. To use the lifetime campaign budget option, you need to calculate the run dates of your campaign. Facebook will then attempt to allocate the budget evenly across the life of the campaign.

The minimum daily ad spend is $1.00 per day. The minimum CPC is $0.01, but you will not get clicks if you bid this low.

The bidding process is very competitive. Your ad will never be seen if you bid too low. When you create your ad campaign, Facebook will suggest a range of what you ought to bid and automatically set your campaign to the highest bid within that range. It is up to you to change the bid.

AVERAGE CPC AND CPM

There are two ways to bid on Facebook: CPC (cost per click) and CPM (cost per mille). You choose which bidding method you want for your campaign. Studies have shown that in the United States, the average CPC is $0.24 and average CPM is $0.66. Put another way, US advertisers pay on average $24.00 to get 100 clicks or approximately 36,000 views. These figures vary widely among industries and advertiser sizes. For instance, large retailers have very high CPMs and CPCs as opposed to food-and-beverage companies.

For local businesses, these costs can be on the high side. For example, a local restaurant's audience is much smaller than the entire country, limited to a city or a neighborhood. You have learned that targeting to a niche market can be beneficial in that these people are more likely to convert. But a small, local audience will have many other local businesses bidding for the same audience. There are also the national advertisers that want everyone. So do not be surprised if your costs are closer to $1.00 CPC and $2.00 CPM.

FEED THE TOP OF YOUR FUNNEL

Increasing relevant likes of your Facebook Page replenishes the pool of potential customers you can lead down the path to purchase. Try to direct these people to the point of choosing to see your content in their News Feeds. This signifies the Consideration phase of the purchase funnel, which increases your chances of getting them to the Transaction phase.

The key is spending money to increase relevant likes of your Facebook Page. You can buy really cheap likes by focusing on irrelevant countries, but that would be just wasted money. The cost of relevant likes will depend on your brand recall and the competitiveness of your industry. Recognized brands, of course, can generate likes at costs that are orders of magnitude lower than those of SMBs. So you need to target your audience very finely.

Generally, expect to reach relevant Facebook likes to cost between $0.20 and $1.00. The rule of thumb here is that the less you spend, the lower your cost per like. That is because you will need to increase the size of your target audience as you spend more, which means that your audience becomes less ideal as you expand.

Bear in mind that the following costs per likes are approximations, but they do provide a baseline from which you can create budget projections:

- $100 = 200 Likes
- $500 = 750 Likes
- $1,000 = 1,250 Likes
- $5,000 = 5,000 Likes

If your budget is $100, focus exclusively on feeding your funnel.

CONSIDER SPONSORED STORIES

Bearing in mind the customer journey, this part of your budget is about increasing your fans' level of consideration of your business. It can be used to drive traffic to your website or to new content on your Facebook Page rather than to drive purchases.

Remember that these ads reach your fans and relevant nonfans in their News Feeds and in the sidebar. One tactic you can employ to optimize your budget is targeting not only your valuable fans in their News Feeds but also relatively less valuable nonfans in the sidebar, which costs much less.

A best practice to follow here is to run these types of ads a few times per week for the whole day. This formula approximately equals a reach of 20 percent of your fans. This reach level keeps your ads beneath the nuisance point—if you try reaching all your fans all the time, they will get annoyed with you. The Optimized CPM (oCPM) for this approach will be very roughly around $5.00.

So with 20 percent reach at $5.00 CPM, here is what you can expect to spend on these types of ads targeting your fans:

- 500 Fans: $0.50
- 1,000 Fans: $1.00
- 10,000 Fans: $10.00

If you want to target nonfans by optimizing your spend on the sidebar, you might find an oCPM of roughly around $0.03 for an audience size of 500,000. So for a single promoted post, the formula for the amount you would pay to reach nonfans might look like this:

- 5,000 Nonfan Impressions: $.15
- 10,000 Nonfan Impressions: $.30
- 100,000 Nonfan Impressions: $3.00

CLOSE THE DEAL

Now you get to the bottom of the funnel. If you still have money in your budget, this is when you promote products and services. At this point you should focus on your fans exclusively. You have invested in them as you led them down your purchase path. They are the ones ready to convert.

Promotional ads for e-commerce should use conversion tracking to target fans and drive them to a landing page on your website or Facebook storefront. If you want to drive people to your physical store, you might offer coupons or other incentives in your ad.

CREATING YOUR FIRST FACEBOOK AD

The easiest thing about Facebook Ads is setting up your account. But to complete the process, you will need to create your first ad. So you must summon everything you have learned and all the work you have done to this point to create an effective ad—defining your target market, creating your value proposition, understanding your niche, writing your messages, and taking great photos. If you have followed the structure of this book, you should have great content and valuable experience in generating organic traffic. You can use those skills to create an effective paid ad for the first time.

Many best practices for paid ads, and Facebook Ads in particular, overlap with recommendations for generating organic traffic. However, there are other best practices that are particular to paid ads. Here is the formula that you should bear in mind while you are making your ads.

MAKING AN EFFECTIVE FACEBOOK AD

At this point, you have learned how to optimize your Facebook Page to drive organic traffic, as well as how to analyze your traffic data to define your audience. Before jumping into creating your first Facebook Ad, it would be helpful to analyze the overriding performance metrics of search ads as the foundation for what makes an effective Facebook Ad. Search marketing introduced CTR (click-through rates) as the success metric for digital ads. So, it makes sense to examine search-marketing best practices as the standard and then compare them to Facebook marketing.

In search marketing, the following three main ingredients are the basis of CTR:

1. *Relevance:* The most effective ad for any search term would be 100 percent relevant to that term. This means more than merely having some or all of the keywords of the search term in the ad copy. It also means the page on which the searcher lands (the landing page) contains the product or service for which the person searched.

2. *Call to action:* This element is designed to create a sense of urgency and motivate a person to click your ad now.

3. *Value Proposition:* This answers the question of why people should choose your store or service over the competition. You should have the answer to this by now.

Effective ads on Facebook share these same elements. The big difference will be your messaging strategy based on the overriding behavior that is different when people are using search engines compared to when they are on Facebook. On search engines, people "pull" information—they search for information and then peruse the search results to find the right website. On Facebook, people check on their online social lives, which means information, for the most part, is being "pushed" to them. So you need to add a pinch of distraction as another ingredient. Your Facebook Ads need to rise above the din to grab people's attention.

It is even more important to bear in mind the best practices of relevance, calls-to-action, and value proposition, along with overcoming the distraction factor, when you create your Facebook Ads.

SETTING UP YOUR FACEBOOK ADS ACCOUNT

Follow these steps to set up your account:

1. *Log into Facebook.* On your personal Profile Page, click the drop-down menu at the top-right corner, and then click Create Ads. Make sure you're on the Advertise on Facebook page.

2. *Choose whether your ad will redirect users to your Facebook Page or a landing page on your website.*

3. *Go to the lower part of the page.* Choose one of the options under "Choose the objective for your campaign"—Boost your posts, Promote your Page, Send people to your website, and so on. Make sure you're on the Design Your Ad page.

4. *Enter a 25-character headline and a 90-character description.*

5. *Upload an image that is 100 by 72 pixels.* Make sure you're on the Choose Your Audience page.

6. *Select the audience that you want to see your ad.* Remember to use what you learned in the Audience Insights section. Make sure you're on the Campaign, Pricing and Schedule page.

7. *Name your campaign.*

8. *Choose how much money you are willing to spend over a specified period of time.* Make sure you're on the Add a Funding Source page.

9. *Provide payment information and specify a period of time for the Ad to run.* You will be billed on a monthly basis. Your ad will be on hold for approximately one day as it goes through the approval process.

PART

3

SUSTAIN YOUR SUCCESS

You set up your Facebook Page and optimized it to generate organic traffic. After that, you learned to use Facebook Insights to track and analyze how your audience engaged with your content. Now that you know how to set up and use Facebook Ads, it is time to understand how to use Facebook Insights to track and analyze your ROI.

FACEBOOK INSIGHTS FOR AD TRAFFIC

ROI is not just about seeing how well your campaigns are driving sales. That is your ultimate goal, but if this is the only metric that has your attention, then your Facebook marketing campaigns will never reach their full potential. You should look at ROI holistically through the lens of the purchase funnel. Along with traditional ROI, you also need to track Social ROI—how you engage with your audience from awareness to consideration. This is how you continually feed your funnel and nurture your audience to the point of sale.

To that end, this section is divided into how to set up and use Facebook Insights to measure Ad ROI (conversions) and Social ROI (engagement).

AD ROI

With Facebook Insights, you can monitor the conversions that your Facebook Ad drives. This is the key to measuring the ROI of your Facebook advertising efforts. This conversion tracking process uses a feature called an "offsite pixel."

To explain how an offsite pixel works, let's say that you ran a Facebook Ad and your sales increased 25 percent. Nice! But just how many of those conversions did the ad drive? What other factors could have helped drive that increase? Conversion tracking traces the people that your Facebook Ad redirected to your website, using the offsite pixel to indicate if those people who were redirected to your website performed the action that you equated to a conversion.

The Offsite Pixel

An *offsite pixel* is a piece of code that you get within Facebook Insights, the installation of which is explained later in this section (see page 90). You insert the offsite pixel within the <HEAD> tags of a Web page that signifies a completed conversion—for example, the Thank You or Success page that people see after making a purchase.

For instance, if the goal of your Facebook Ad was to sell a product on your website, Facebook would track the person who clicked the ad to your website because of the offsite pixel. With the offsite pixel living on your product's Thank You or Success page, Facebook can track if that person lands on it, which would signify a conversion.

Conversion Types and oCPM

An important advertising term with which you are already familiar is CPM (cost per mille). This means how much you pay for every one thousand views of your ad (*mille* is Latin for "thousand"). It is the basis of how traditional and digital advertising is purchased. In terms of conversion tracking, Facebook uses oCPM to decide which people get to view your ad.

The oCPM algorithm that Facebook uses is designed to serve your ad to the people whose profile and past actions make them the likeliest candidates to act on your ad's call to action. Ideally, this goal keeps Facebook users happy with the ads that they see and allows you to get the best ROI from your ad budget. At least, that is what the system is designed to accomplish.

The offsite pixel just discussed allows you to optimize your ad for the following types of conversions:

- Adds to cart
- Purchases
- Leads
- Page views
- Registrations
- Custom conversions that you define

Setting Up Your Offsite Pixel

Follow these steps to generate an offsite pixel:

1. *Go to the Power Editor.* At the top-left menu, click Conversion Tracking.

   Click the Create Pixel button.

2. *Name your pixel and select a conversion category.* This is the action on your website for which Facebook will optimize your ad.

   A box containing code will appear. This is the offsite pixel.

3. *Copy the code.*

4. *Paste the offsite-pixel code inside the <HEAD> tags of the Web page that signifies the conversion.*

   How and where you paste the code depends on two factors:

   - Your website's content management system (CMS) will determine how you implement the code.
   - The Web page in which you implement this code depends on the action that signifies a conversion for you.
     - » Adds to cart: the Web page after Add to Cart
     - » Purchases: the Web page signifying a successful checkout
     - » Leads: the Thank You page after the contact form
     - » Page views: the Web page that you want viewed
     - » Registrations: the Web page signifying a successful registration

5. *Refresh the Web page after you install it.* Facebook will then know that it is active.

6. *Verify the pixel is Active.* In Power Editor, your new pixel will appear in a list as one of the following:

   - *Active* means that people have viewed the Web page containing the pixel within the past 24 hours.
   - *Unverified* means your pixel may not have been installed properly because no data is coming from the Web page in which you installed the pixel.
   - *Inactive* means no one has viewed the Web page containing the pixel in the past 24 hours.

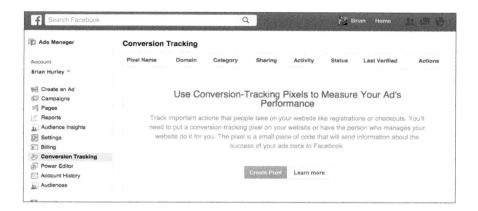

FIGURE 18

FIGURE 19

7. *Analyze your conversions.* Facebook Ads Manager will give you the following statistics about your ad:

- *Conversions:* The number of times the offsite pixel was activated
- *Conversion Value:* The value of your conversions based on your definition
- *Cost Per Conversion:* The average cost of your conversions

To figure out your campaign ROI, divide the cost per conversion by the overall costs of the product (production costs, shipping costs, inventory costs, etc.).

SOCIAL ROI

When most business owners talk about measuring ROI from ad campaigns, they usually mean using immediate sales as the performance metric. The purchase funnel tells us that there is a path people take toward making a transaction. Getting people on that path is integral to the success of your business. Much of Facebook marketing revolves around these "softer" metrics. Spending hard money on soft ad campaigns whose goal is increasing long-term engagement with your audience can be problematic to quantify.

When you create a social ad, start by selecting an objective that drives an action signifying engagement—likes, shares, and comments. Then use Facebook Insights to track these actions and analyze their social impact on your business.

Next, you will learn how to measure and analyze the Social ROI of your Facebook Ads. This information will help you assess their value to your business and identify which ads work best.

Measuring Social Engagement

When you choose to run Marketplace Ads to drive likes or to advertise using Sponsored Stories or Page Post Ads because of their reach, you use Facebook Insights to track the social impact of your campaigns. So the same metrics used to track and measure organic traffic also apply to paid traffic.

Compare organic likes to those driven by ad campaigns. Then, compare the paid likes to the ad campaigns that occurred during that time to calculate their contribution to new likes. This figure represents their social ROI value.

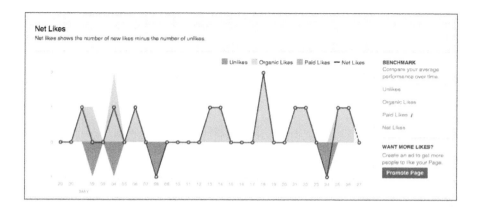

FIGURE 20

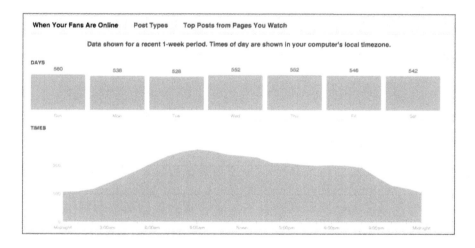

FIGURE 21

You also can see the level of paid reach that you achieved from boosted and promoted posts and compare that number to organic reach. You can view reach statistics—as well as post clicks, likes, shares, and comments—in the Posts tab in Facebook Insights.

Click the post itself to get detailed information about its engagement and reach.

To calculate social ROI, divide the money spent by the number of engagement actions. For example, if you spent $10 and the return equaled 250 likes, you generated 25 likes per dollar. Now it is up to you to figure out if the campaign was worth the investment for your business.

Assess the likes, reach, and engagement that you generated through ad campaigns. Evaluate them against the campaigns you generated through organic methods. Doing this analysis allows you to identify which campaigns are worth the money. This knowledge is vital to planning your future Facebook marketing strategies.

REMARKETING TO AN INTERESTED AUDIENCE

This is a tactic available through Facebook Ads that lets you advertise to people who have visited your website. It is Facebook's version of *retargeting*. This happens when visitors see an ad on one website, then days later, the same ad reappears on a completely different site.

That explanation should give you an indication of Facebook Remarketing's power and also its downside. Think about visiting a website for reasons other than commercial ones, or maybe you already bought an airline ticket or booked that hotel. Then you see ads for those websites while browsing another website. This experience can seem illogical . . . or even creepy.

Remarketing can increase conversions and decrease overall cost per acquisition, so it is a powerful ad feature. But as with any type of power, overusing it can backfire. This problem is generally the concern of large companies for the reasons explained above. For SMBs, people usually visit your websites because they are looking for what you have to offer. Still, be careful how you wield this power.

Luckily, there are features that allow you to focus on those website visitors who express more interest in what you have to offer than others. Remember, you can remarket to people who have visited your website that have not yet made a purchase, existing customers who have made a purchase, and people who have not visited but have shown interest.

Now that you have learned how to let Facebook track visitors to your website and how to create audience segments, you can use this knowledge and skill to remarket.

Lower Cost Per Click

Facebook Audience Insights lets you create hypertargeted audiences. This capability can drive traffic that is as relevant as, yet less expensive than, search traffic. Facebook users who have visited your website but have not converted yet are one example of this. Remarketed Ads usually have lower costs per click than normal Marketplace Ads for this reason.

The messages that you create for remarketing must be different from the copy that you create for your ads in general. Think about including additional information that people might not get from your website. This contributes more value to the ad experience than merely regurgitating your overall messaging.

Make the Sale the Second Time

As the purchase funnel illustrates, converting first-time visitors to your website into customers is a path that takes time. As a consumer yourself, you check out multiple websites when you are shopping. You will visit a website, go off to another one to compare prices, and sometimes you forget the name of the first one if you have closed the tab.

Remember, you can create focused custom audiences. In order to remarket to website visitors who have yet to buy from you, create a custom audience around those attributes. You can exclude people who are existing customers to target only new consumers who have shown their interest by visiting your website. And when this audience sees your well-crafted ad on Facebook, you have a better chance of becoming recognizable, which increases your chances of completing the purchase cycle.

Remember to avoid using this tactic too often, as there is a point where remarketing of this kind becomes a nuisance.

Profit from Social Proofing

There are benefits to including existing customers in your retargeting strategy. When current customers are allowed to interact with potential ones, they often share positive comments about your business. Current customers are also more prone to engaging with your content than new consumers. When new consumers see those comments through remarketing ads, it provides "social proof" of the trustworthiness of your business, which can help drive sales.

Furthermore, the connections that remarketing drives with current customers can increase brand loyalty. Keep in mind that loyal customers are more valuable to your long-term success than new ones. They will continue to buy from you at minimal cost per acquisition. When current customers see your company on Facebook, there is a good chance that they will advocate your brand to other users. The likelihood that they will buy from you again is also much higher than that of new customers.

Remarket to Shared Characteristics

Remarketing allows you to go beyond people who have visited your website to those who share characteristics with them. These are called Lookalike Audiences. These people very likely are interested in your products or services because they have similar traits to the people who have either already bought something from you or have landed on your website during a search. Lookalike Audiences provide you the opportunity to reach relevant potential customers that you were missing out on and who are also likely to be interested in your product or service and will ultimately convert.

PROMOTIONS: GIVE TO GET

Promotions are one of the best ways to interact with and promote your business to both new and regular customers. They work at any stage of the purchase funnel—awareness, consideration, transaction, and loyalty.

Your first goal always should be to get a visitor to your Facebook Page to take action by liking or sharing it. Next, your objective should be to get them to return to your Facebook Page and interact with your business on a regular basis. Promotions help in accomplishing just that.

PROMOTIONS IN ACTION

It is one thing to have the technical knowledge to run contests and understand how to abide by Facebook's rules governing promotions. But it is an entirely different thing to create a promotion that meets your business objectives. So here are a few ideas to get your creative juices flowing.

Encourage sharing through mobile devices. A simple competition that helps drive sharing can work well if the content that you ask people to share is visually appealing. Doing so through mobile devices means you can reach your current and potential fans more easily and more often.

If you sell stylish items that people treasure, you can run a competition in which people enter by registering their e-mail addresses and other details. Then, let them choose their favorite stylish item among similar items and share their selection to their friends. Sharing stunning photos over mobile devices creates tangible engagement. This practice has the potential to circulate easily if the friend happens to be with another friend in real life, not just on Facebook.

Let your consumers be the stars of the contest. If you sell products that people can wear or a professional service that packages people's talents, give your consumers an incentive by featuring themselves in photos or videos and uploading them to enter your contest.

Photos and videos are very engaging, and uploading them encourages people to stay on your Facebook Page longer, which is the very essence of brand engagement. Also let fans comment on the uploaded content and share their favorites with their friends.

Make winning the contest itself the prize. If you are a nonprofit or a for-profit business co-marketing with a nonprofit, giving away prizes can be difficult to justify against your bottom line. So consider making the prize the game through a leaderboard based on collecting some sort of action.

People can provide their digital signature for a petition supporting a worthy cause and also be given the ability to invite their friends to sign the petition. A dynamic leaderboard on your Facebook Page can keep a running tally showing who is collecting the most friends to sign the petition. Those watching themselves climb the leaderboard have a strong incentive to do more sharing. Everyone feels good about themselves, but the winner feels the best.

Connect with people wherever they may be. Your existing and potential customers use different devices and social media networks throughout the day. So, having the ability to run your competition across devices and channels simultaneously means you can reach them wherever they may be.

Consider creating a contest that allows participants to enter by uploading photos, videos, and text through Facebook, Instagram, Twitter, and texting. Put the entries into the content gallery provided by a third-party app, with Instagram and Twitter entries identified using a campaign hashtag.

If you are going to run such a sophisticated campaign, make sure it is optimized for mobile devices.

Survey your discerning customers. If your product or service is meant for a very discerning market segment, you can use a thematic interactive quiz to attract relevant customers.

For example, you can create a quiz that only connoisseurs of your product would be able answer (or would take the time to answer) and give away a valuable package of your products. Require entrants to opt in to receive further information about your tasteful offerings, including their e-mail addresses, so you can nurture them through your sales process while using Facebook Ads to promote the quiz to new customers.

Let your consumers tell you what they want. If you create handmade products or provide customized services, a competition that asks for your consumers' input can be a compelling way to get them involved in the creation process. This approach provides multiple benefits in terms of helping you create things that people want while inspiring them to market for you.

Consider having contestants submit their ideas as the rule for entry into the contest. Leverage multiple entry points by embedding the contest app on your website and Facebook Page. Allow others to vote on what they think are the best ideas to engage those who might not want to submit their own ideas but still want to participate in the event. Use a third-party app that automatically captures the participants' demographics, location, and contact information so you can reach your target group with customized offers.

Let your fans stuff the ballot box. Encourage your fans to promote your promotion for you by giving them a higher chance of winning for doing so.

The tactic here is to give contestants multiple entries as they get more people to enter the competition. For example, give away a prize that your audience would find valuable and that you can afford to give away on a weekly basis. When people sign up, they are required to give their e-mail addresses and then asked to share the contest to their friends. To make this request compelling, the contestant can be offered multiple automatic entries for every one of their friends who signs up as well. The combined act of sharing and a resulting action increases their chances of winning, all the while driving your contest's exposure.

CONTESTS AND SWEEPSTAKES: GET IN THE GAME

Generally speaking, you can think of *contests* as games and sweepstakes as *lotteries*. Running a contest on Facebook is a powerful way to generate awareness and increase your number of fans. But as with any game, you need to know the rules to have a chance to win. Facebook has strict rules around the types of campaigns you can promote.

There are two ways to run contests on Facebook: using the features built into Facebook or using a third-party app to manage your contests. Facebook has limited the functionality of its built-in promotions features in order to constrain their liability. Nevertheless, starting out using Facebook's features will allow you to gain experience in running contests. As you ramp up your knowledge, hone your technical skills, and figure out the types of contests that work most effectively for your business, you can graduate to using third-party apps to administer your contests.

CONTESTS USING FACEBOOK FEATURES

These ads show up directly on people's Timelines. Users are able to comment on your post in order to win something, or they can like a photo to win a contest. These types of contests are designed to drive engagement with your current Facebook fans. Because these features are built into Facebook's, they are much easier to set up than contests that you manage through third-party apps. Plus, you do not have to pay the third-party app subscription fee.

Of equal importance to devising the most effective contest for your type of business is knowing the related rules and regulations governing their use. Otherwise you can be penalized by having your Facebook Page taken down. Seriously, do not risk running a contest without understanding how to adhere to Facebook's rules. Even though Facebook does not have enough resources to monitor every promotion out there to catch rule breakers (and there are a lot), consider this: All the time, care, and resources that you have invested in your Facebook Page might be lost if you get caught and your Facebook Page is taken down.

Facebook's promotion rules state that the methods for gathering entries from users to your Facebook Page comprise the following:

- Posting directly about the contest
- Messaging about the contest
- Commenting on the post about the contest
- Liking a post about the contest
- Liking to vote on a piece of content

For instance, you can create contest entry rules that require users to comment on your post, message you about the contest, or upload a photo on your Facebook Page. Then, you can choose a winner based on which submission garners the highest number of likes, randomly select a winner, or even require that entrants answer a question that you have posed.

Although there are many actions on Facebook that you can use as entry requirements, there are a few that you are forbidden to require of users to enter contests:

- Tag themselves in a photo that does not show them
- Share a post
- Post to their own Timelines or to friends' Timelines

COMPLYING WITH ALL APPLICABLE RULES AND REGULATIONS

You need to follow Facebook's rules. Also be sure to comply with the local regulations of where you do business, define your contest rules and provide easy access to them, and release Facebook from any liability that may arise from your contest.

Facebook's Promotion Rules

You are solely responsible for the lawful management of your promotion, including the following:

- Following Facebook's official rules
- Being aware of any terms and conditions governing your promotion and all prizes offered

Local Rules and Regulations

You are responsible for complying with all regulations of the country, state, province, county, and city in which you do business. It is solely up to you to research and understand any limitations of running contests and sweepstakes that may apply to you based on where you do business.

Your Promotion's Official Rules

You must draft the official rules for your contest or sweepstakes and make them easily visible and accessible to your participants.

- Your rules must state explicitly the types of prizes that you are offering and the manner by which the winners will be selected and contacted.
- You should publish these rules on your website and on a tab on your Facebook Page. That way, you can link to the rules within your post, thus showing proof that the rules of your contest were plainly accessible to participants.

Release Facebook from Liability

The timeline post announcing your contest must incorporate Facebook's legal language regarding promotions on Facebook, which includes the following:

- Each entrant's complete release of Facebook's liability
- Each entrant's acknowledgment that Facebook is not administering, associated with, sponsoring, or endorsing your promotion.

CHEATERS CAN MAKE YOU LOOK BAD

Verifying legitimate entrants or votes for your contest or sweepstakes is difficult. Would-be participants can create fake Facebook profiles. Their strategy is to enter numerous times or to take part in a conspiracy to exchange votes with co-conspirators with a view to increasing their chances of winning.

In contests based on taking a quiz, understand that participants have the ability to correct their comments. That makes it unfeasible to identify which answers in the comments were originally correct and which ones were corrected after seeing other participants' answers.

You might read all these warnings and think, what's the big deal? As long as someone wins, the contest generates buzz for your business, and ultimately increases sales, then it was a success. Not exactly, because if your contest has unclear rules and someone ends up winning who was not a legitimate participant, you might have to face disgruntled fans. They will fall out of the purchase funnel and most likely never become loyal customers. Word spreads quickly in social media, and your brand equity might take a big hit.

As much as you can, make certain that your contest draws honest contestants while identifying and addressing fraud. In this endeavor, you can partner with legitimate entrants who often are the first ones able to spot the frauds. When fraud is brought to your attention, address it quickly and decisively.

THE RIGHT WINNER FOR THE RIGHT TIME

You can pick the winner of your contest at random, sort through comments and pick out the first correct answer, or examine posts to uncover the one with the highest number of votes. All these methods will take some time, with the first option taking the least amount of time.

You are not using a third-party app that can pick the winner automatically based on preprogrammed rules. So, you will need to evaluate the amount of time that you can invest in this endeavor while still being able to operate your business.

SOMETIMES DECENT IS BETTER THAN FABULOUS

The real reason for holding a contest on Facebook is to motivate people into doing something on your Facebook Page. In order to achieve this, you will need to serve consumers something of value. You do not necessarily need to offer major prizes to lure people. The prize just needs to be something they find valuable.

If you can afford to offer a fabulous prize, this isn't necessarily better than giving a decent prize. Here's the reason:

- Offering a Hawaiian vacation as a prize will engage your participants and cause them to monitor and scrutinize how you pick the winner. They will use their judgment to see if you are doing this fairly. If your selection process is not clear and, therefore, is open for interpretation, you can face a virtual riot on your Facebook Page.

- Offering a less fabulous yet still valuable prize, like a dinner and movie for two, will generate interest. You can manage this easily in terms of participant scrutiny, and it will be more affordable for your business.

SUCCESS STORY

It's All Good—Cause Marketing with the Collage

CASE STUDY ADVERTISER PROFILE
NAME: The Collage
TYPE OF BUSINESS: Independent hair salon
MONTHLY FACEBOOK AD SPEND: $500

Businesses looking for a ways to bring goodness to their venture and to benefit something greater than themselves traditionally have integrated corporate responsibility and cause-marketing programs. *Cause marketing* refers to a type of marketing that involves cooperative efforts between a for-profit business and a nonprofit organization for mutual benefit. It is broadly used to refer to any type of marketing effort for social and other charitable causes, including the stand-alone marketing efforts of nonprofit organizations. Cause-related marketing differs from corporate giving, which usually involves a tax-deductible donation. Cause marketing involves an in-kind relationship.

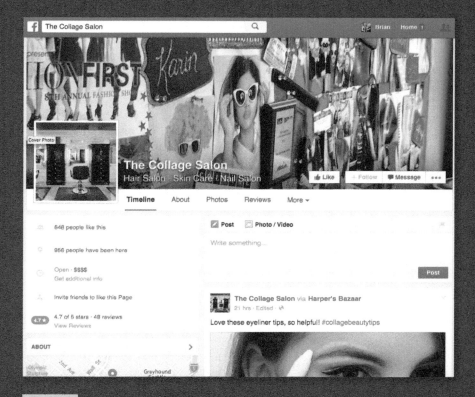

FIGURE 22

Cause marketers have turned in increasing numbers to Facebook, which makes a lot of sense. When marketers want people to know about the good that they are doing in the world, Facebook is the prime platform for this. These types of activities work well in social media because it is a space where people expect to be engaged in this way.

Maybe it is because of our shared human experience that makes social media, and Facebook in particular, a natural fit for cause marketing. Social media propagates human-to-human contact on a large scale. That is the same reason that people join causes.

STAND OUT BY STANDING UP FOR SOMETHING: The Collage is a hair salon based in the Belltown neighborhood of Seattle. A multifaceted family of artists occupy their sleek, bright, and meticulously crafted space. They looked for ways to increase awareness of their brand, which they had positioned as both organic and stylish. The Collage wanted people to know what makes them stand apart from their competitors:

- Employees are treated like family.
- Staff members are appreciated as artists.
- Customers love the overall experience.

Being a small business in a highly competitive industry, they did not have a marketing team or large budget. They were marketing on Facebook, because that is where the majority of their current and potential clients spend most of their time online. As much effort as possible went into optimizing their Facebook Page to drive organic traffic, as well as running a few ads. Still, like all small businesses, they could have used more.

The owners of the Collage thought that aligning the business with a cause they were passionate about and carrying out a co-marketing campaign would support the essence of their brand. They realized that this effort could also make them outshine their competitors. The owner was aware that Facebook had become arguably the premier channel to carry out cause-marketing efforts. So, creating a campaign that would be marketed through Facebook seemed like the natural thing to do.

DO THE RIGHT THING FOR YOUR BRAND: Just because cause marketing and Facebook fit like hand in glove does not mean any charitable campaign will be a success. Back when Facebook had only hundreds of millions of users (rather than 1.4 billion currently), campaigns offering a $1.00 donation in exchange for a like of a Facebook Page was cutting edge. Nowadays those types of campaigns seem as unsophisticated as Myspace. Furthermore, just because a business wants to form a mutually beneficial cause alliance to co-market on its Facebook Page does not mean any nonprofit will be amenable. Some nonprofit organizations reserve Facebook opportunities for their long-term partners.

When approaching a nonprofit organization for a marketing partnership, small business owners need to ensure that it will be a good brand fit. Then they should come to the table with creative ways to provide value that fits the nonprofit's mission. Equally, many small businesses do not have the resources to sponsor marketing campaigns in which they give a donation for a Facebook action. In this situation, small businesses have to find clever ways to provide something that will be worthwhile to the cause other than straight-up cash.

The owner of the Collage had an association with a charitable organization called the Justice and Soul Foundation. The founders both had come from the fashion and beauty industry. They created the foundation to focus on the awareness and elimination of sexual exploitation of young women and children globally, as well as the restoration of the survivors.

A VIRTUOUS CYCLE OF MARKETING GOODNESS: Justice and Soul planned to host an event that was a combination fashion show, auction, and fundraiser. Proceeds from the event would go toward the foundation's operating budget and building a cosmetology vocational school in Cambodia. That last part is key to their mission—it includes the restoration of trafficking survivors through teaching formal skills that support their independence. A few of the artists from the Collage, some of whom were also burgeoning fashion designers, would show their hair and clothing designs at the event. So the Collage pro- moted the event on its Facebook Page.

The content was not merely a copy of the flyer that Justice and Soul were handing out. Emphasis was placed on the fact that proceeds would be allocated to building the cosmetology school. The online universe at once makes people feel closer together yet farther apart. Therefore, it's important to point out how even the smallest action translates into a real-world difference. In any cause- marketing campaign, it is not enough to say that your actions have caused a donation. Stories move people to action.

The event sold out for the first time. It was such a success that Justice and Soul announced on their own website and Facebook Page that they are looking for a larger space for the event next year. They anticipate accommodating twice as many people. The event also generated brand awareness for the artists of the Collage who participated in the show, while giving the business itself the luster of goodwill.

CONTESTS USING THIRD-PARTY APPS

Now that you have gained experience in running contests and sweepstakes using Facebook's built-in features, you can take your operations to the next level: Use third-party apps built for managing Facebook promotions. These are the most popular types of contests run on Facebook. They allow you to leverage entry forms to collect e-mail addresses and further information about contestants.

Here are the main advantages of using third-party apps to run your contests.

Grow your e-mail database. Having the ability to communicate with your fans on your Facebook Page is valuable. However, it is not that same as being able to directly communicate with existing customers through e-mail. Using a third-party app allows you to collect the e-mail addresses of your players with an e-mail opt-in on the contest entry form, thus converting fans into a database that you own and can monetize.

Capture data about your fans. Data about existing and potential customers provides you with the ability to generate qualified leads for your business. Running a contest through a third-party app lets you gather data on your fans. This is important in understanding whether you are attracting your target market or if there are other customer segments that you should be targeting.

Encourage referrals. Referral features give your contest the power to increase the amount of participation in your contests. These features take advantage of the viral nature of social media to expand your reach well beyond your current fan base.

Drive conversions. Third-party apps give you the ability to offer contestants a special offer or coupon in exchange for their entries. This can be used to drive foot traffic for local businesses, while giving your fans an added benefit for entering your contest.

To capitalize on the features that third-party apps offer above and beyond Facebook's built-in functionality, acquaint yourself with the ones most widely used. A list and description of the most popular contest apps, along with ones that offer time-saving features for managing your Facebook campaigns, can be found in The Facebook-App Ecosystem section of this book on page 109.

THE FACEBOOK-APP ECOSYSTEM

Throughout this book, you have seen from time to time the word *ecosystem* describing the network of Facebook's apps. Now is a good time to clarify this term.

An *ecosystem* is any grouping or network of interconnecting and interacting parts. Originally, the word described the interaction between a community of organisms and their environment. When you think about Facebook's 1.4 billion users, 54 million business pages, and 7 million connected apps and websites, then you can see a living, breathing thing.

Facebook's social graphs and expressions have become the nearly universal index of personal connections and preferences. And you do not need to log into Facebook to be on Facebook—Instagram and WhatsApp are mere doorways into Facebook. To a certain extent, so are Twitter and YouTube, if you have linked your accounts.

As a Facebook user, you can sometimes feel overwhelmed by the convenience and choice of it all. As an SMB, you can capitalize on all these doorways and entry points. But as your business and your marketing acumen grow in parallel, you will need a way to automate and streamline your processes before you get overwhelmed.

So here is a list of Facebook apps for business to help you move forward. Short descriptions for each one give you an overview of their respective value propositions. That way you can identify which apps you might need at certain junctures of your marketing evolution and then research those further.

CONTEST APPS

These are the apps that you will need to run contests and sweepstakes requiring features that go beyond the ones built into Facebook.

Antavo: Along with the contest features, you also get integration with games and loyalty programs. Furthermore, the customer insight features are sophisticated.

Pagemodo: Allows you to create contests, cover photos, custom tabs, as well as design and schedule posts.

ShortStack: This app works more like a central hub for social commerce than merely a contest app, but it has many contest features available for you to use.

SnapApp: This program is designed for interactive contests, meaning you can offer more ways to engage your audience than just static opt-in forms.

Wishpond: This contest app has many different types of contests for you to use, including contests based on votes, hashtags for networks outside of Facebook, captions, and music contests.

Woobox: This one is used by more than three million different companies, so it is trusted based on its pervasiveness. You can run almost any contest that you can imagine.

APP SUITES

These programs offer many more features than the contest apps, though they offer those features as well. As your marketing efforts become more complex, these app suites can help you manage robust campaigns.

Agorapulse: This suite does most everything you need to manage your Facebook Page, along with other social sites. Comes with deep analytics and reports, including competitive analysis.

Cision: This company merged with Vocus, which had acquired North Social beforehand. So if you run across articles mentioning North Social, it is Cision now. These machinations resulted in one of the strongest social management platforms in the industry.

Heyo: Known for its mobile capabilities, this suite of apps allows you to create templates for just about anything that has to do with Facebook marketing, including contests and tab pages.

Ripe Social: Allows you to make tabs, create portfolios, offer coupons, produce videos, manage Twitter/Facebook synchronization, and create RSS feeds.

TAB APPS

These are the apps you should turn to when you want to create a unique tab on your Facebook Page. You can integrate your other social accounts or media sources with Facebook using these apps. You can also use them to create customized frame-based Web pages to use as landing pages.

SocialAppsHQ: This one is brimming with features and is the choice of some of the biggest brands in the world, which means it can be somewhat complicated to use. It offers deep analytics and integrates with your website and Facebook Page.

Tabfusion: A well-known brand within the Facebook-app ecosystem, this app lets you make tabs to cover all your marketing needs. And you get a two-week money-back guarantee.

TabSite: Also used by some of the biggest brands, this program lets you make tabs for contests, coupons, and videos. It eases the decision to purchase the app with a 14-day free trial.

SCHEDULING APPS

For all you busy entrepreneurs who do not have time to manage your Facebook Page, these apps allow you to queue your posts months in advance, coordinate engagement tactics, and manage spam. Using these apps means you will need to plan your strategy and tactics in advance, and then invest further time in setting up the programs. Performing these tasks up front will pay off in the long run. Doing so will free you up to manage your social media campaigns.

Hootsuite: The most popular campaign manager across Facebook and Twitter, this dashboard provides so many conveniences, including scheduling messages and measuring ROI, that they cannot all be listed here. There is a paid Pro version available for serious social media managers, but SMBs will be able to do everything they need with the free version.

Post Planner: The fact that this app is free—though you have to pay to use higher-level features—means it is also a good choice to start your foray into scheduling apps.

E-COMMERCE APPS

These apps allow you to turn your Facebook Page into an e-commerce site. For those of you who do not have e-commerce capabilities on your website, doing so through your Facebook Page is a good way to get your feet wet in e-commerce. These apps sometimes make it easier for you to integrate these capabilities than it would be on your website.

Those of you reading this book who already have the facility to sell online through your website might see this section as superfluous. Help your Facebook fans by providing them with a method to buy from you that decreases the number of clicks required from your Facebook Page to your website. This practice can increase your conversion rate.

PayPal

This is the easiest method to allow people to pay you from your Facebook Page, so the steps to set up this functionality are included here. You can use this payment method to test the consumer response to your venture into e-commerce. Then you can decide if you need to integrate other e-commerce apps that provide more sophisticated features. You will need to have a PayPal account already set up.

1. ***Create your payment link.***
   - Log into your PayPal account. The Button Creation page appears.
   - Fill out the information for your product's name, price, and item ID (if you use one). Do not add any drop-down menus or text boxes in the Customize Button section, as they will not work with a text link.
   - Click Create Button at the bottom of the page. You will be redirected to the button code page.
   - Click the E-mail tab located above the box with the code in it.
   - Click Select Code, which automatically will highlight the code in the box.
   - Right-click the highlighted code; a submenu will appear, then click Copy. Or you can press Ctrl+C for Windows or Cmd+C for Mac.
   - Now go to Facebook and log into your account.

2. *Share your link as a status update.*

- Post the link to all of your friends as a status update by right-clicking your status update box and clicking the Paste submenu item, or you can type Cmd+V on Mac or Ctrl+V on PC. You should include explanatory text in your status about what people would be buying when they click the link.

- Click Share and the link will show up in your status. When people click the link, they will be redirected to the PayPal payment page for that item where they can complete their purchase.

3. *Add the link to your About Me or Info section of your Facebook Page.*

- On Facebook, click Profile.
- Click Info.
- Click the Edit button next to Basic Information.
- Right-click and select the Paste submenu item to enter the link into your About Me section, or you can type Cmd+V on Mac or Ctrl+V on PC.
- Click Save Changes. Now when customers come to your Facebook Page, they can click your Info to copy the link and paste it into their browsers to pay you. Note that the link will appear only as plain text instead of as a dynamic link.

4. *Add your link as a Note.*

- On Facebook, click Profile.
- Then click Notes.
- Then click Write a Note.
- Type a title for your note in the title field, and then paste the link into the body. Include an explanatory message with your link, and then click Publish.

Ecwid

Ecwid is arguably the most popular shopping app in the Facebook ecosystem. It is a safe to say that its freemium plan, allowing businesses to use it free to sell up to 10 products, has driven its high-adoption rate. There also are no setup or transaction fees, so other than the PayPal link, it is the fastest way to start selling on Facebook.

Just because the service starts out free does not mean it is limited. It works with a variety of content management systems and other e-commerce platforms. Moreover, it integrates with an assortment of shipping carriers, including FedEx, UPS, the United States Postal Service, DHL, Canada Post, and even Australia Post.

Shopify

This is a collection of apps that you can use on more than 100 store templates. Shopify has many features that other solutions do not offer, such as a free card reader, unlimited SKUs, and discount codes at checkout. Its premium plan offers further features to optimize for conversions. Competing solutions would force you to integrate with a different third-party solution to get access to these types of features.

Shopify's collection of apps allows you to decorate your Facebook store with accessories like coupons, competitions, and even a help desk.

ShopTab

This solution offers one of the simplest interfaces of all the e-commerce apps, so it is attractive to SMB owners. But it is also a robust solution that some of the biggest brands in the world use to run their Facebook stores.

Features include the ability to select how many of your products that you want to present on your Facebook store page, like-gating (requiring people to like your page so that they can shop), mobile shopping, and localization support of international currencies and languages.

Storefront Social

Storefront Social is not only popular among established brands, but it is also the e-commerce choice of many SMBs. Like StoreYa (covered next), it can integrate with many third-party providers. Although there are no free features to start, there is a seven-day free trial.

Storefront Social does not have the same selection of features as other Facebook e-commerce apps. What makes it an attractive solution are its capabilities, such as simple connection to Twitter, Google+, and Pinterest; multicurrency and multilingual support; and data-feed integration with Google Base Feed, Yahoo Commerce Central, and CSV files. Moreover, it is mobile friendly.

StoreYa

For SMB owners who already have or plan to have a presence on eBay, Etsy, Amazon, and WordPress (through WooCommerce), StoreYa makes it easy to integrate and import your digital storefronts to your Facebook Page.

StoreYa's e-commerce–marketing tools include features like a coupon pop-up to use as an incentive for your fans to check out your Facebook store, a collective purchasing mechanism à la Groupon, and even a scratch-and-win coupon game.

The cool coupon pop-up is the only feature available with the free plan. If you're a small business in the beginning stages of e-commerce, this is a cost-efficient and scalable way to grow your online business. After that, monthly plans based on your inventory size kick in.

Vendevor

Easy setup of your online store within minutes and credit card–processing capabilities makes this solution a popular choice with SMBs. Because the app offers credit card processing and supports bank transfers, it provides a substitute to PayPal for those of you who would rather not accept PayPal payments.

Unlike many other Facebook e-commerce apps, enabling coupon codes is available only at the higher tier plans, so the service has its limitations.

Stand-Alone Apps

The aforementioned apps provide multiple social campaign and e-commerce–management features, whereas these apps are designed to perform one specific task.

Contact Tab: The website may look a bit sparse, but it belies a dynamic piece of software. It may not be as feature rich as other apps, but that is because it was designed to do one thing and do it well: create contact pages. It is also free to use.

Fan of the Week: Allows you to pick a random fan every week who you can feature on your Facebook Page. Works well for small audiences who like being recognized.

LiveChat: You can offer live chat functionality directly on your Facebook Page without relying on Facebook's messaging system.

NetworkedBlogs: You can allow multiple blogs to publish through your Facebook feed.

PollDaddy: Rather than having to use links to other survey applications, you can run polls directly from your Facebook Page.

RSS Graffiti: Make a specific tab in which you can curate blog content through an RSS feed on your Facebook Page.

10 MISTAKES TO AVOID

Facebook Marketing for Small Business has shown you how to implement the same Facebook marketing techniques that industry experts use. But sometimes knowing how *not* to do something is just as important as knowing how to do it. Here is our list of the 10 most common Facebook marketing mistakes. Avoid them all, and you'll be that much closer to mastering Facebook marketing.

1. DO NOT AVOID COMPLETING YOUR FACEBOOK PAGE

Starting out with the obvious, make sure that you set up your Facebook marketing efforts for success by completely filling out your Facebook Page. If you took shortcuts during the section that explained how to set up your Facebook Page, stop reading now and go back. You should have included your hours of operation, address, photos, website address, and your value proposition in the About section. Otherwise people cannot gather this information quickly. Not doing this will hinder everything else that you do for your business on Facebook.

2. DO NOT IGNORE COVER PHOTO GUIDELINES

Your Cover Photo is the first thing that people notice, so it should abide by Facebook guidelines:

- No price or purchase information, including discounts
- No call to action to like, share, comment, download, get it now, or tell your friends
- No contact information, like Web, e-mail, or mailing address

If you think about it, these things would just make the Cover Photo look cheap. Instead use an image that showcases your product and portrays your brand essence. And do not forget to change your photo once in a while—this practice refreshes your brand image and allows you to promote a new or different product, an upcoming event, or a new location.

3. DO NOT SELL

This advice may seem contradictory to marketing, but it is the number one mistake perpetrated in social media marketing.

The majority of businesses that make the mistake of directly promoting sales in their posts are new to Facebook. They approach it in the same way as traditional marketing, like flyers and print ads. It is an approach that makes people cringe.

For those of you who have any experience with business-development cycles, you know that selling big-ticket items or complex solutions takes a long time. It is not about just getting the transaction; it is about building a relationship based on the trust that comes from being an expert advisor. Successful Facebook marketing requires the same thoughtful approach.

The reason you want to market on Facebook is to promote your products or business in your Facebook posts. However, you need to do it indirectly—as the trusted advisor of the community you have built or in an entertaining way.

4. DO NOT USE TOO MUCH TEXT

Facebook posts and ads need to be bite-sized morsels that can either be consumed as a stand-alone snack or serve as the appetizer that gives people the appetite to click a link to a bigger meal of content.

Remember to write your posts like a tweet. Following Twitter's 140-character limit forces you to distill your idea to its essence, making it easy and simple for people to read and understand what they get from having read it. Do not inundate the short attention span of your audience with multiple calls to action. Instead have the discipline to constrain your little poem to one call to action to achieve one goal.

5. DO NOT IGNORE COMMENTS, ESPECIALLY NEGATIVE ONES

Your work has just begun after launching your post or ad. You need to monitor your posts to assess the level of engagement and to respond to user comments. You need to show every comment in which someone asks a question, makes a suggestion, or provides negative feedback respect by responding to all of them, except for quick comments like "I love it!" or "I do that too!"

Remember the video United Breaks Guitars? Just one unattended negative comment can spread like wildfire, undoing all your goodwill and community-building efforts.

6. DO NOT BEG FOR LIKES AND SHARES

Likes and shares are the main currency of Facebook. But asking people to like and share your post straight-out without offering anything in return is just plain begging.

Liking and sharing are the mechanisms that people use to engage with you, but engagement is a two-way street that offers people the opportunity to take an enjoyable or useful journey. Otherwise it is just spam.

7. DO NOT OVERPOST

The rule of "less is more" applies here. You should start your Facebook marketing efforts with one or two posts per week to assess what works. When you ramp up your posting frequency, bear in mind that industry experts have found that posting more than once per day can decrease engagement. Facebook studies point out that the average user likes four to six new Pages every month, so the competition for attention is fierce. With so much content inundating Facebook users, posting one outstanding piece per day instead of two passable ones will give you a better chance of standing out.

8. DO NOT POST BORING OR IRRELEVANT CONTENT

Just because people like your Facebook Page does not mean that all of them share your interests as well. Avoid posting things that are not relevant to your brand just because you think they are cool. Staying on-brand is a major predictor of engagement, so give people a mix of content related to your product or service, rather than your lifestyle. Unless your business sells a lifestyle product or service, then by all means leverage that lifestyle component because doing so means you are staying on-brand.

Since your fans do not see every one of your posts, you risk wasting their attention on irrelevance and potentially suffering negative engagement.

9. DO NOT BREAK CONTEST RULES

It is imperative that your Facebook contests follow Facebook's guidelines and local laws. The rules change every so often, so staying on top of the fine print can be time consuming.

You can find Facebook's guidelines here: www.facebook.com/page_guidelines.php.

10. DO NOT IGNORE FACEBOOK INSIGHTS

If you do not know which of your marketing efforts are working and which are off target, then you are wasting your time and money. That is the exact formula for going out of business.

But you will not fail to track and analyze the performance of your Facebook marketing efforts, right? Because you are ready for this. Now go get 'em.

RESOURCES

The Collage: www.thecollagesalon.com

Do Us a Flavor Contest: www.dousaflavor.com

Facebook Business Overview: www.facebook.com/business/overview

Facebook Help: www.facebook.com/help

Facebook Statistics: www.statisticbrain.com/facebook-statistics/

Google AdWords Keyword Planner: adwords.google.com/KeywordPlanner

HubSpot Blog: blog.hubspot.com

Instagram Business Guide: www.business2community.com/instagram/
set-instagram-business-guide-01165005

Justice and Soul Foundation: www.justiceandsoul.org

LikaLove: www.likalove.com

Linking PayPal to Facebook: www.paypal.com/webapps/mpp/get-started/
add-payment-link-to-facebook

Mobile Optimization: streetfightmag.com/2015/03/19/
small-businesses-and-the-impact-of-mobile-optimization

Pew Research Center's Social Media Update 2014:
www.pewinternet.org/2015/01/09/social-media-update-2014

Purchase Funnel: o2ointeractive.com/understanding-the-purchase-funnel
-from-online-to-offline-and-back-again

Saleforce's Social Advertising Benchmark Report 2014: www.salesforce.com/
form/marketingcloud/social-ads-benchmark.jsp

Social Media Examiner: www.socialmediaexaminer.com

United Breaks Guitars: en.wikipedia.org/wiki/United_Breaks_Guitars

INDEX

MAKE
THE INTERNET
YOUR ASSET

EARN MORE WITH

'NET WORTH
Guides

 TYCHO PRESS

Also available as eBooks

CPSIA information can be obtained
at www.ICGtesting.com
Printed in the USA
BVOW07s2238111216
470262BV00006B/6/P